The Co-Creator's Handbook 2.0

The Co-Creator's Handbook 2.0

An Experiential Guide for Discovering Your Life's Purpose
and Birthing a New World

Carolyn P. Anderson
Co-created with Katharine Roske

Additional copies of this book can be obtained in the U.S. for $22.00 plus $4.00 shipping and handling. For each additional book, add $1.00 for postage, except for bulk orders or bookstore purchases, for which discounts are available. California residents add 8% tax. Overseas residents, please contact connect@globalfamily.org for cost of shipping. You may use check, PayPal, VISA, or MasterCard. **To order additional copies: http://www.globalfamily.org.**

Global Family
17738 Minnow Way
Penn Valley, CA 95946 USA
connect@globalfamily.org

ISBN: 1883208033
ISBN: 9781883208035

Library of Congress Control Number: 2016911263

The Co-Creator's Handbook 2.0: An Experiential Guide for Discovering Your Life's Purpose and Birthing a New World

By Carolyn P. Anderson with Katharine Roske

Edited by Carolyn and Sanford Anderson
Cover by Trina Brunk
www.globalfamily.org
www.cocreatorshandbook.com

*The mission of Global Family is to empower and connect individuals
and groups to actualize their purpose and co-create positive change in the world.
Offering the Core Group Process™ is foundational to our mission.*

What others have to say about
The Co-Creator's Handbook 2.0

By consciously learning the practices that are offered in The Co-Creator's Handbook 2.0, we are making an immeasurable contribution to this quantum jump to the next stage of human evolution—to "heaven on earth." This guidebook provides us with personal and social processes whereby we can make the jump together, from the inside out, from our spiritual motivation and unique creativity outward, bringing ourselves into new forms as co-creators of the magnificent new world that we know is possible.

> Barbara Marx Hubbard
> Author of *Conscious Evolution, Emergence,* and
> *52 Codes for Conscious Self Evolution*

I believe that working in groups creates transformational synergy, that we can travel faster and deeper together than we can travel on our own. Through the evocation of one another, we expand the base of our concern, developing an enhanced relationship to our planet and intensifying our recognition of its needs as well as our willingness to respond creatively to those needs.

Working in community, each person holds the dreams and excellence of everyone else in the group, so that should we descend into a period of depression or despair, our excellence and dreams are held by the group until we return to a healthier mindset. And if we can do this for each other, we can hold as well our collective dream for the world's future.

> Jean Houston,
> Author of *Jump Time* and *A Passion for the Possible*

We cannot heal the Earth by acting from feelings of fear and isolation. To build a sustainable and meaningful future, we must learn to tap into our inner creativity and then join with others in a spirit of compassionate service. The Co-Creator's Handbook is a book by pioneering social architects who practice what they preach. This book provides an inspiring map for the journey from discovering our inner creativity to developing a supportive and synergistic community and then to practical and cooperative actions in the world.

Duane Elgin
Author of *Promise Ahead* and *Awakening Earth*

Contents

Contents

Dedication

To the One appearing as many............
and to the many who are playing their parts in birthing a new, more loving world.

For Lucky —
My friend, soul-sister
and co-creative partner.
With much love and
appreciation —
Carolyn

Acknowledgments

THE IDEAS AND practices offered in this book have been woven from many threads over the past few decades. We gratefully acknowledge the following friends and colleagues for their generous contribution to our lives and to this work.

Barbara Marx Hubbard—visionary, social architect, and evolutionary thinker—has been our friend, co-creative colleague and mentor for decades. Her pioneering work with the Core Group Process™ has laid the foundation for this *Handbook* and inspired people around the globe. Her friendship and guidance has touched our hearts and expanded our awareness. We acknowledge Barbara and her Foundation for Conscious Evolution for the innovative work they are doing to shift consciousness on the planet.

Our sincerest heartfelt gratitude to our devoted husbands: Sanford Anderson and Makasha Roske for their loving support and wise counsel. The joining of our genius is a continuous source of joy, inspiration, learning, and deepening.

Special thanks to Marion Culhane for her vision and commitment in co-founding Global Family, for her on-going support and inspiration, and for being the kind of sister that only the fortunate few can claim as kin!

We are grateful to Carolyn's late husband and co-creative partner John Zwerver who, as editor of the earlier version of this book, contributed so much to the content and spirit of this work. Thanks, too, to Tim Clauss for years of devoted service to Global Family, for his invaluable contribution to birthing Core Groups around the world, and for co-creating many of the tips, principles, and exercises in this *Handbook*. We laud his talent and generosity of spirit and treasure his friendship.

We extend deep appreciation to our Hummingbird Community in New Mexico for modeling co-creation and serving as a living laboratory for the evolution of consciousness. Special thanks to Rich Ruster, Ralph Huber, and David Fischer for the leadership roles they have taken in educating others about co-creative practices.

Marian Head, Amaeya Rae, Lila Tresemer, Juan Carlos Kaiten, Louis Bohtlingk, and Alan and Dianne Collins have been most generous in sharing their brilliance with us in the form of experiential exercises or exploratory dialogues. May their kindness and selflessness be returned in surprising and meaningful ways many times over!

And, finally, we thank our children, grandchildren, and future generations for leading us across the threshold into a new world of unity and love.

This has truly been a co-creative endeavor, and we are deeply touched by the support we have received from so many people who mean so much to both of us.

With love and appreciation,
Carolyn Anderson and Katharine Roske

The Call

THIS IS AN invitation to participate in perhaps the greatest adventure of all time . . . birthing a new world . . . a co-creative society.

Just as many of our ancestors often traveled great distances to be able to fully express their beliefs, ideals and thirst for freedom—we, the social pioneers of our time, are being called from within to manifest a new culture that reflects the expanded awareness that we are experiencing in our lives.

The old forms, structures, and institutions no longer serve our collective needs as we are inspired to take responsibility for co-evolving our world. At this auspicious time in our evolution, there stirs within the hearts of a growing body of humanity the yearning to discover and model new social forms which honor unity and diversity and call forth each individual's full creative potential.

As our consciousness shifts from separation and fear to unity and love, we desire to join with others in co-creative endeavors that embody the values and virtues of trust, respect, equality, cooperation, equanimity, humility, generosity, integrity, and compassion.

This is a new horizon—a journey into uncharted territory. Many have come before who have pointed the way, responding at moments when the cry from the confused masses echoed around the world. The great masters, saints, and prophets have exemplified what is possible. Most have walked a solitary path, being misunderstood and often persecuted.

Now, at the time of the Great Turning, social pioneers are realizing that we need not walk alone. As Thich Nhat Hahn so eloquently expressed, "The next Buddha may not be an individual, but an enlightened community." We move from a consciousness of "I" to an awareness of "we" as Whole Beings, serving one another in a process of mutual awakening. At this time, millions of courageous individuals in towns and villages around the world are opening to a greater reality by responding to a cry in their hearts to take the inward journey to "know thyself." This creative minority is now sufficient in number to shift the tide.

Emerging from an early wave of social innovators, *The Co-Creator's Handbook 2.0* is a response to the need for a transformed society. This guidebook offers processes, tools, experiential exercises, and understanding necessary to support individuals in expressing their heartfelt purpose and bringing forth the kind of world many dream is possible. It is the evolutionary imperative of our time to join in teams, create and maintain a field of love, align collectively with Spirit, and bring into manifestation new social forms that embody an awakened consciousness. Collectively we have the inherent genius, the boundless creativity, and the abundance of resources necessary to respond to the vast challenges of our times.

This invitation goes out to all pioneering souls who are realizing their essential nature, all who are responding to an inner call, all concerned with the absolute well-being of life. May we be bold, courageous, and innovative as we collaborate in birthing a new world, a co-creative society in service to the highest good of all.

On behalf of all life and future generations to come, let us take the evolutionary leap and embark on this transformational journey together.

Foreword

By Barbara Marx Hubbard

THERE IS EMERGING a new humanity that holds within itself the seeds of a radically new future, one that has been envisioned in the great mystical traditions of the human race: the new heaven, the new Earth, and the New Jerusalem—beyond death, beyond scarcity, beyond the illusion of separation between humans and the Divine.

It is my sense that we are living through a period of quantum transformation and that on the other side is this radically new future which has been envisioned, yet relegated to the purely mystical or the afterlife. This future is actually the attractor of the next stage of human evolution. It is now unfolding in our midst, not as life after death, but as life after this stage of life. Revelation is unfolding in evolution. We have reached the end of one phase of human growth and consciousness and are entering a new era toward an emerging future still unknown.

It is becoming clear that self-centered humans with powers to transform life—in our current state of consciousness—will no longer be viable. Through biotechnology, nanotechnology, robotics, artificial intelligence, and quantum computing, humans are gaining ever increasing powers to destroy the existing world. We are facing a choice: either extinction or conscious evolution. This amounts to the evolution of evolution itself, from natural selection to conscious choice. If our species can learn ethical evolution in our generation—if we can attune to the deeper reality itself like the great seers and mystics of humanity have always done—we see the possibility of an immeasurable and unknown future: cosmic consciousness, species transformation, and contact with other life. If not, we already see the possibility of our own extinction.

In this epochal change toward the next stage of evolution, three great streams of evolution are unfolding: The New Story, The New Person, and The New Society. *The Co-Creator's Handbook 2.0* makes a critical contribution to each of them.

The New Story is the universal story of our evolution from the origin of creation to the First Age of Conscious Evolution. We are the generation to become aware of evolution and to realize that we are affecting it by everything we do. This means evolution by choice, not by chance. We are facing the daunting challenge of *how to evolve consciously*, not only to avoid self-destruction but to foster conscious self-evolution toward a future that attracts us. Humanity has no training in this field. Here is where this *Handbook* offers vital guidance.

The New Person could be called Homo Co-creator. This person is universal in consciousness: one who is embodying within the deeper process of creation, the Impulse of Evolution, the divine intent of universal creativity. This person is awakened by a passionate desire to participate in giving his or her gift, in becoming more loving, more creative, and in being an actual expression of the tendency toward more conscious life. This *Handbook* supports us to evolve as Homo Co-creator.

Next comes The New Society: The Co-creative Society. There is an emerging culture now arising in our midst that expresses the qualities of this new person who is *already* dedicated to restoring Mother Earth, to freeing humanity from injustices, conflict, war, and disease. Homo Co-creators are humans guided by their soul essence, tending toward cosmic consciousness and visions of a world in which all people are free to give their best.

The Co-Creator's Handbook 2.0 has divined the design of conscious evolution! The essence of this design is allurement, joining together in a field of love to co-create. Nature has been joining seemingly separate parts into ever more complex whole systems for billions of years. Now humans are beginning to do it consciously.

As described in this book, individuals join together in Co-creative Cores to fulfill the potential of each person and each group so connected. They do so by attraction in a field of resonance. *These small groups are the structure of the new world already arising in our midst.*

The *Handbook* places this design into a number of deep yet simple processes that take us from small groups learning to build the field of resonance and shared insights, through a series of practices that reveal the pattern of self and social evolution. The process culminates with

Co-creative Cores connecting, synergistically, through shared life purpose to develop new systems, innovations, and projects for the emerging world.

Core Groups are formative units of the emerging culture. As they connect and manifest action through the chosen vocations of their members, they are even now becoming organic functional elements within the new social body—its healers and entrepreneurs, its communicators, educators, artists, managers, and leaders of all kinds. Even now, networks of human-scale communities composed of such small resonant groups are forming the basis for the cultural reformation of the world.

Taking a deep breath and jumping across the quantum abyss in our imaginations, we can already see the glimmers of a radically new world. We have developed a society whose organizations are co-creative with the patterns of evolution and with the spirit of creation in each of us. When we begin to add to the processes of social synergy new interactive internet capabilities to connect us co-creator to co-creator, our planetary nervous system will begin to become coherent. Facebook, Twitter, over seven billion cell phones, Google, and other dedicated platforms are gradually organizing to support co-creation.

As our planetary nervous system is infused with co-creativity and love—and new structures such as Core Groups connect us with one another—the collective consciousness of humanity is being uplifted.

Into this emerging technological and social arena, we can see young co-creators, our children's children, entering into the process of conscious evolution. We see them designing new social systems and eventually gaining access and guidance over the evolutionary technologies which promise radical new powers, abundant energy, and non-polluting technologies to liberate us from Earth-bound, creature human existence. Even now we find ourselves at the threshold of universal life.

Core Groups practicing the essential elements of co-creation are a home base for pioneering souls who are called to make the transition in our own lives, families, work, and communities. By modeling this change personally and socially, at whatever level we are capable of, we are seeding the chaotic culture around us with islands of coherence and alignment with the deeper tendency of evolution for higher consciousness and greater freedom through a more synergistic order. We are making the quantum leap ourselves. When we are resonating together in this mode, we are living *in this very moment* in a new heaven and a new Earth. Wherever two or more are gathered in this state of being, the future is present now. We realize the dream and fulfill the promise of all the great mystics of the world.

By consciously learning the practices that are offered in *The Co-Creator's Handbook 2.0*, we are making an immeasurable contribution to this quantum jump to the next stage of human evolution—to "heaven on earth." This guidebook provides us with personal and social processes whereby we can make the jump together, from the inside out, from our spiritual motivation and unique creativity outward, bringing ourselves into new forms as co-creators of the magnificent new world that we know is possible.

Gaining the Most from This Handbook

THIS GUIDEBOOK HAS been created to support the evolution of individuals and the formation of co-creative groups who have, or wish to develop, a shared purpose or project. It is a tool to empower you to learn the principles and practices of co-creation and to support you in finding your teammates so that, together, you can evolve yourselves and the world. Those groups that have had some previous experience in building trust and attaining resonance will get even more benefit from this guide, as it will lead your group to the next step, which is co-creation.

The groups and communities that can benefit from learning co-creative practices include businesses, intentional communities, families, shared households, focused teams, action groups, church and service groups, and any other small group that comes together to experience personal evolution and healing or to support positive change in their community and in the world. Thousands of pioneering souls have discovered that putting these essential elements into play facilitates individual and collective transformation.

The Core Group is not an emotional support group. Its function is connection, not correction, experience not observation, emergence not emergency. Participants must have attained a basic level of psycho-spiritual maturity to desire to move beyond their personal story, join their unique genius with others, and contribute to the birth of a new society.

Handbook Overview

SECTION 1 OF the book offers an overview of the essential elements of co-creation and provides a context for the process.

SECTION 2 offers instructions and materials to guide you in forming and maintaining your Core Group.

SECTION 3 is the heart of the matter. It consists of a series of exercises that your group can experience to fully empower yourselves. To gain the most from these experiences, we strongly encourage each member of your group to buy a *Handbook* and to read SECTIONS 1 and 2 before moving on to SECTION 3.

SECTION 4 provides a glossary, the co-author's biographies, and information to stay connected with a number of innovative organizations and with the growing community of co-creators worldwide.

Many of the guided meditations that are offered in the *Handbook* have been recorded and can be found at www.cocreatorshandbook.com. As you move through the chapters, you will see which ones are recorded here. We invite you to visit this site to share your wisdom, comments, and insights as you experience the Core Group Process™ with your group, so that we can learn from one another.

We, the co-authors, are committed to the ongoing development and sharing of best co-creative practices. To this end, we will occasionally publish supplements to the *Handbook* that reflect these advances. The publisher will notify subscribers to the Global Family mailing list as new downloadable files are added. *If you would like to receive these notifications, please join the mailing list at www.globalfamily.org.*

You will probably need many meetings to experience all the material provided in each chapter of this guide. Do not rush through the exercises in an attempt to "cover more ground." Savor the joy of building group resonance and the privilege of being fully present to the process of self-discovery and group empowerment.

Most of the exercises are meant to be approached in a linear fashion; that is, you can start at the beginning of the each chapter and move through every process or co-create your own version of the exercise. Circle 5 on ceremonies and rituals is an exception. We suggest that you go through this chapter before your second or third meeting to become familiar with the contents. You can then use the practices as the occasions arise.

The essential ingredients of this process are the love and awareness each person brings to the group. Creating and maintaining resonance allows each element to emerge spontaneously in perfect timing.

If your group is entering the process as a Co-creative Core, you might read through the introductory material and experience a few of the processes in the first few chapters, and then proceed to Circle 7.

To facilitate the reading of this book, the pronouns he or his and she or her are used interchangeably in referring to both men and women.

To ensure a feeling of safety and to support deep communication and maintain trust, please remember that personal sharing is to be held in confidence by all members of your circle.

An Invitation to Co-Creation

An Invitation to Co-Creation

ARE YOU YEARNING to fulfill your soul's purpose?

Do you feel called to share your gifts in resonance with others?

Are you inspired to play your part in birthing a new, more loving world?

If so, you are being lifted up from within by an energy as powerful as the drive for self-preservation or self-reproduction. It is the longing for Self-realization and Self-actualization. It is this alignment as our authentic selves, linking with others who share our vision and "passion for the possible" that creates positive change in the world.

We call it the urge of co-creation. It is the uprising of human creativity, an evolutionary force that can transform the world. As we collectively move into this new territory, we are finding our way together. There are no maps and few mentors; the only true guides reside within us. We are discovering the process together, following our intuition, and learning as we go.

We are at the threshold of a global renaissance that has only been dimly dreamed of by the visionaries of the human race. Each of us has the potential to awaken as our Authentic Self, discover our soul's purpose, and join with others to birth a new world, a co-creative culture!

The Evolution of the Core Group Process™

———— ❧ ————

THE PRINCIPLES AND practices that are shared in this book have been revealed over time to a number of groups around the globe. Indigenous people have practiced many of these elements for centuries; however, before Global Family's publication of the original *Rings of Empowerment* guidebook, no one had ever described the full model or presented it as a whole system so that it could be replicated by others.

The essential elements of this process were revealed to Barbara Marx Hubbard and Carolyn Anderson in 1984 as they toured the U.S. for Barbara's Vice Presidential Campaign for a Positive Future. People formed spontaneously in small circles, attracted to the vision of a better world and the roles they might play in creating a new society. They developed resonance and joined genius with one another as they became dedicated to serving the vision and mission of the Campaign. It was by mapping the pattern of the Positive Future Centers that the outline of this model for personal and planetary transformation was discovered and the process was revealed.

As co-founders of Global Family in 1986, Barbara and Carolyn developed the concept of the Core Group Process™ and initiated early trainings to share the model with others. When Tim Clauss joined the staff of Global Family in 1988, he worked with Carolyn to co-create many of the exercises, tips, and guidelines that are contained in this book.

In those early years, the word "co-creation" was not in the dictionary. Although members of Findhorn Community had used this word to describe their relationship with nature, most people were unfamiliar with the basic concept. Barbara Hubbard and Global Family were instrumental in making the term popular through their publications, trainings, and gatherings in the 1980's and 1990's. Today, "co-creation" is in the common vernacular and is often used in business to mean cooperation or collaboration. Seldom, outside of a relatively small number of groups and organizations, is it used as defined in this *Handbook*: "conscious alignment with Source, nature, and the essence of Self and others; creating consciously with the Impulse of Evolution."

In 1996, a Core Group of six members of Global Family—including Carolyn and Katharine Roske—co-founded Hummingbird Community, bringing co-creative practices and the worldview of conscious evolution into the community. Continued application of the practices has cultivated a coherent resonant field that is strong, stable, and evolving.

According to Barbara Marx Hubbard, *"Hummingbird is the first community dedicated to conscious evolution and co-creation. It represents the heart and soul of the co-creative movement."*

At one point, the elements of the Core Group Process™ were referred to as the "Rings of Empowerment." Later, in the original version of the *Handbook*, the co-authors renamed the model the Circles of Co-Creation. We believe that the elements of these Circles are the essentials that are required to liberate human creativity and shift society from a hierarchical to a partnership model.

The term "Resonating Core Group" refers to a small group of people who practice relating to each other from a center or core of unconditional love and authenticity. Whether they are called "Core Groups," "Wisdom Circles," or "Evolutionary Circles"—any small group that provides the safe space to relate to others from a feeling/heart place and encourages the full expression of intuitive knowing is a type of Resonating Core Group. It is in the resonant field that individuals begin to shift their consciousness from an "I" to include a "we" focus and experience the value of tuning into the collective intelligence of their circle.

"Co-creative Cores" are an evolved form of Resonating Core Groups. They are groups that have come together around a shared purpose that actualizes the gifts of all members and contributes to the betterment of society. *Unlike groups that focus on personal and spiritual growth but don't take social action in the world, and unlike social action groups that don't take the time to cultivate harmony and resonance among themselves, groups that follow this template model love and action.* Co-creators choose to use their work and their relationships with one another as the way to design the world they choose. Co-creative Cores are an evolutionary leap in social organization and a new structure for personal and group empowerment. In their highest form, they demonstrate that their project or activity is a vital piece in the pattern of the whole.

By seeding our organizations and communities with these synergistic social units, we can become fulfilled, actualized humans who are making immense contributions to society. As members of co-creative groups, we can drop the old habits of fear, dominance/submission, unhealthy competition, and separation. In their place, we can experience love, harmony, cooperation, and alignment that will greatly increase our effectiveness in creating positive social change.

An Overview of the Circles of Co-Creation

THE ELEMENTS OF co-creation offer a series of practices to assist you in stabilizing as your Authentic or Essential Self, discovering your life's purpose, and joining with others to birth a new world. The following is an overview of the Core Group Process™.

Each Circle, as described in Section 3, contributes an element of this process and presents inspiration, information, and experiential exercises to evolve and empower you and your partners. When all of the elements are practiced consciously, genuine transformation occurs and there is an increase in awareness, creativity, and fulfillment. Awakening as co-creators, we become the change we want for the world—giving birth to a culture that more truly reflects our values, vision, and consciousness.

The graphic below is a two-dimensional depiction of a process that is evolutionary, dynamic, and transformative. The center represents love, Spirit, and the Self. Each of the other "Circles" surrounds the center, is informed by the center, and works synergistically with all the other Circles in a non-linear manner.

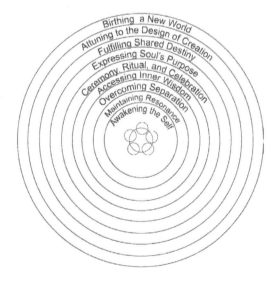

Circle 1: Awakening the Co-creative Self

Common to all traditions and belief systems is the evolutionary impulse to "know thyself." Through grace, and in divine timing, each of us embarks on a sacred journey of inner exploration and becomes more aware. We awaken as presence or loving awareness and begin to embrace all aspects of our being—the light and the shadow. Gradually, our identity shifts from our personality self to our Authentic Self (or Self), and we experience a feeling of deep inner peace and all-pervading love. We realize that the Impulse of Creation is expressing through us, *as us*. This movement into action as the Authentic Self is the awakening of the Co-creative Self. Our being shines through our doing and we become true co-creators, universal intelligence incarnate—the "new person."

We recognize that each of us is unique *and* universal. We share common needs for creative fulfillment and the experience of community. We evolve from self-centered to whole-centered consciousness and are drawn to kindred souls who share our passion for allowing the love that we are to find full expression. Like caterpillars, we move out of the cocoon of false identity to experience ourselves as butterflies. We stop searching and start celebrating life as it presents itself, moment by moment.

Circle 2: Creating and Maintaining Resonance

Love is the fundamental unifying and creative force in the universe. As we connect at the heart and hold each other in unconditional love and acceptance, an invisible field is created. It is this resonant field of love that supports us in accessing the creative force, giving birth to the co-creative process.

When we are truly seen, accepted, and acknowledged for who we are, our trust is deepened and we feel empowered. We practice non-judgment, forgiveness, and loving one another as ourselves. We use every incident as an opportunity for reflection, transformation, and healing. Our life is our work, as we embody the principles of resonance minute by minute, on a daily basis—in our workplace, our homes, and our communities.

Circle 3: Overcoming the Illusion of Separation

Coming together in this unified field of profound harmony, intimate sharing and safety, our feelings of separation and fear begin to dissolve. We face and eventually embrace our

An Invitation to Co-Creation

imperfections and learn a set of communication skills that support alignment with our true natures. We create agreements that encourage authenticity, call forth our potential, and empower each of us to fully express our unique creativity. Practicing forgiveness, we are able to build trust, dispel the illusion of separation, and acknowledge the truth and beauty we see in one another.

Circle 4:   Accessing Inner Wisdom

As we rest deeply in a field of love and trust, an opening in our consciousness naturally occurs. The "still, small voice of God," the wisdom that resides in each of us, reveals itself through deep listening. The whispers of the Essential Self becomes audible as we slow down, turn our attention inward, and honor our innate wisdom.

The resonant field of our Core Group lifts all of us and supports our unique creative expression and wholeness. Together, we gain greater access to universal intelligence. We learn to trust our hearts, follow our inner guidance, and receive the love and support of those who are sharing this journey of awakening with us.

Circle 5:   Ceremony, Ritual, and Celebration

We develop ceremonies and rituals to help anchor and maintain the state of resonance and to make our relationships sacred—to each other, to the Earth, to all life, and to Spirit. Aligning with the natural order, the cycles of the seasons, and the phases of our lives—we take time for retreats, rites of passage, and periods of silent reflection. The ordinary becomes sacred as we breathe meaning into the mundane and embody the wisdom that we are.

Having come home to our Self, we express our potential in concert with nature and others; we trust the moment and celebrate what wants to happen.

Circle 6:   Expressing Your Soul's Purpose

It is the destiny of each of us to awaken to our true nature and to discover and express our unique calling. We discover our true place by following the wisdom of the heart and going within for guidance and direction. We learn to "follow our bliss," our "compass of joy." We call on the co-creative intelligence of our group to assist us in refining and reflecting upon our soul's calling.

9

As our divine destiny reveals itself, we seek to join our mastery with others who share our deeper purpose, in order to magnify our collective genius and better serve the needs of the whole.

Circle 7: Fulfilling Your Shared Destiny

Once we are aware of our unique purpose, we are drawn to others who are aligned with our values, vision, and mission in order to fulfill our shared destiny. In Resonant Core Groups the shared purpose of the participants is to focus on the evolution of its members. Co-creative Core Groups commit to projects and activities that actualize the unique purpose of all members of the group and allow each person to participate fully and equally. We enter a state comparable to marriage, deepening our intimacy and committing ourselves to be faithful to our partners and our agreed upon actions.

Spirit is configuring us into groups and teams so that we can play our parts in creating a new culture. Like cells in the body, we are guided to our perfect place in society. Our barometer of success is the sense of joy and fulfillment that is intrinsic to expressing our individual and collective potential.

Circle 8: Attuning to the Design of Creation

As we stabilize as our Essential Selves, strengthen our ability to access our inner wisdom, and join with others who are doing the same, we tap into the field of co-creative intelligence. Our intuitive minds begin to work in concert with our analytical intellects and a new capacity is born. Revelation joins with thinking, and we experience group synergy and the ability to attune to the design of creation.

A new form of governance and decision making emerges. We evolve beyond consensus decision making and access whole-systems knowing. We allow for decision and right action to be revealed. Led by the self-organizing laws of nature, we observe "what wants to happen." A dynamic of synergy, synchronicity, and telepathy is experienced, inspiring us to give form to our collective wisdom. Revelation joins with thinking to support us in governing ourselves as one living system. We begin to stabilize as Whole Beings, attuning to the pattern of creation and sharing our collective wisdom for the good of the whole.

Circle 9: Birthing a New World

It is the nature of love to give back, inspiring the offering of one's unique creative talents for the benefit of all. As our lives are fulfilled, we are naturally inclined to serve: bringing the experience of resonance, love, and inspired insights to the world. This may take the form of an entrepreneurial venture, a philanthropic gesture, a social initiative, or a political movement. Win/win practices ensure that the magnificence and mastery of all participants are honored and brought forth to benefit all members of the team and society as a whole. Giving back in the form of conscious investing, philanthropy, social entrepreneurship, tithing, and gifting become part of the new caring economy.

As institutions and structures break down and new ones come to the forefront, dominance is replaced by partnership. Society undergoes a whole-system shift. New models that reflect an integration of feminine and masculine virtues and whole-centered consciousness are emerging at this time. The feminine values of sharing, caring, nurturing, and embracing become intimately interwoven with the masculine traits of focused purpose and action in the world.

Qualities of the co-creative culture include conscious alignment with divine intelligence, the manifestation of our soul's calling, service that is mutually beneficial, reverence for all creation, deep listening, empowered leadership, and spiritually-motivated social action.

In order to build a sustainable future, all social pioneers are being called upon to evolve personally and to courageously step forward and express their unique gifts in concert with their teammates. As we explore new ways of living, we are birthing whole systems and new structures to express our values and fulfill the destiny of each member of our human family. As Cores converge with one another, co-creators are connecting worldwide to birth a new world.

The Promise of Co-Creation

AFTER PUTTING INTO practice the essential elements of co-creation, we take what we've learned in the intimate safety of our Core Groups and courageously apply those principles to all aspects of our lives: our homes, churches, organizations, and places of work. As social innovators we are choosing to design new forms that bring forth the best in each of us for the betterment of all.

When groups come together in a field of love, safety, and mutual trust—the creativity, power, and wisdom of each person is liberated. The sense of separation within people that leads to war, crime, pollution, and disorder is healed. As each person finds her place in the body of society, every field of endeavor is taken to a higher level of expression. Thus, business, medicine, education, technology, science, and the arts are going through a profound transformation at this time. The pyramid structure is giving way to the circle and ordinary citizens are being empowered to express their full potential. Domination is giving way to partnership. Outer authority is succumbing to inner knowing. Core Groups are emerging to support and empower personal and planetary transformation.

By aligning one group with another, we tap the power and resources available in each Core. Teams link with other teams for the empowerment of all. Eventually, as Cores converge and synergize with one another, a sufficient unified field is built, which jumps the entire system to a new level. All of humanity, all life on this planet, shifts to a higher level of consciousness and we evolve as a species, capable of healing all sense of separation and co-creating the reality we choose. As conscious beings—aware of the cosmos as a living, interconnected, evolving, intelligent reality—we place our attention on manifesting the harmonious integration of our spiritual, social, and scientific/technological capacities on this Earth and beyond.

The task of showing whether or not humanity
is viable rests with us—each of us.
Unlike other species, humanity can anticipate the future,
make conscious choices and deliberately change its own destiny.
For the first time in the whole history of evolution,
responsibility for the continued unfolding of evolution
has been placed on the evolutionary material itself.
We are no longer passive witnesses to the process,
but can actively shape the future.
Whether we like it or not, we are now the custodians
of the evolutionary process on Earth.
Within our own hands lies the future of this planet.

PETER RUSSELL

Models that Offer a Context
for this Process

Spiral Dynamics [1]

ANY DISCUSSION OF co-creative practices is enhanced by an understanding of the work of Don Beck and Christopher Cowan, who built on the work of Dr. Clare W. Graves to offer an evolutionary-developmental model of worldviews called Spiral Dynamics.

The Spiral Dynamics model refers to broad patterns of thinking as memes. (A meme is an idea, belief or belief system, or pattern of behavior that spreads throughout a culture by repetition. Each meme embraces certain beliefs, social groupings, dynamics, and goals.) In this system, these memes are presented as a series of eight levels in two tiers, although it is generally accepted that at least one other level is emerging at this time. Each level represents a stage of human and cultural evolution—a different paradigm.

In this model, it is understood that situations encourage different memes to come to the forefront. For example, the events of 9/11 called forth basic survival instincts for many residents of New York City, calling out the Beige Meme in large numbers for a brief period of time. In addition, an individual might rely on one meme in his work domain and another meme in his close relationships.

The eight memes are listed here with a range of elements that reflect that worldview. Each meme has emerged historically (and within individuals) in response to the needs of new, more complex life situations. First tier survivalist thinking is already giving way to second tier global thinking—even though second tier is practiced by a minority of cultures and individuals.

FIRST TIER

1. Beige: Beige includes those people who operate from basic survival instincts, acting much as other animals, in loose, clan-based survival groups. They may be found in

---

1 Much of this overview is adapted from the work of Steve Dinan of Esalen Institute. The statistics that are offered are his.

isolated cases in the jungles of the Amazon or other remote areas. Famine and epidemics might lead to people operating in this mode. Examples might include the mentally ill, late-stage Alzheimer's, the homeless, and those who feel that their survival is being threatened at the moment. The focus here is on the individual. It is believed that Beige represents only .1% of the world population.

2. Purple: This consciousness supports tribal groupings, a focus on rituals, and belief in magic, connection to the Earth, and the cycles of nature. Change is embodied in ceremonies, traditions, and symbols. Individuals at any stage of the spiral of memes may call on the purple meme to express ceremonially. For example, solstice and equinox ceremonies and rites of passage exemplify the purple meme, which focuses on the group. It is estimated that less than 10% of the world population expresses primarily as this meme.

3. Red: This meme is characterized by rugged authoritarianism, exploitation of unskilled labor, suppression of natural human tendencies, and self-centered consciousness. Red businesses or groups are run by a boss with a strict division of authority. ISIS, Al Qaeda, the mafia, and gangs operate in this meme. Red is represented by approximately 20% of the world's population.

4. Blue: This meme is authoritarian, purposeful, and patriotic. Blue level consciousness emerges as a response to Red meme consciousness and leads people to obey authority and support "law and order." It works well in industrial economies and pyramidal organizations. Examples include all fundamentalists, right-wing conservatives, and religious hierarchies. The focus is on the group. Blue is represented by almost 35% of the world's population.

5. Orange: This level is entrepreneurial, success oriented, and focused on personal achievement and advantage. Motivations are largely economic and it is believed that competition improves productivity. Silicon Valley, Wall Street, and Fifth Avenue in New York City exemplify this meme. The focus is on the individual. Orange is represented by less than 25% of the world's population—who hold disproportionate power in the world.

6. Green: Individuals operating at this level focus on community and personal growth, equality, and democracy. Often they give attention to environmental concerns and value openness, trust, and egalitarianism. Leaders become facilitators and, in valuing equal representation, must navigate group process skillfully to avoid inefficiency and stagnation. John Lennon's music, Ben & Jerry's, Occupy Wall Street, Black Lives Matter, and eco-villages are examples of this meme. The

focus is on supporting the success of the group. Green is represented by less than 10% of the world's population.

SECOND TIER

Second-tier thinking embraces and integrates all other levels and represents a leap in consciousness. It accepts that each level of development is part of the next higher level of development and believes that you can't leave any of them out: their existence is necessary. There is a capacity to hold, respect, and synthesize multiple perspectives. It acknowledges that the best course of action and the best structures can be radically different in different situations. It is accepted that all humans grow and develop thru these stages of consciousness. Second tier embraces a holistic approach to knowing and, in organizations, drops job titles that are so important to Orange-meme consciousness.

Up to this point, all points of view, or memes, were at odds with one another. Second-tier consciousness accepts that all other levels are true but partial and that each worldview has value, given the right life conditions. (For example, it is appropriate to operate from Beige basic survival instincts if you are in a violent situation!)

7. Yellow: With this meme, there is a quantum shift as the individual views life from multiple perspectives, and the orientation is towards integration of complex systems. This worldview likes change and challenges and is characterized by systems thinking: how parts interact to cooperate and create a greater whole. Yellow likes complex ideas, such as chaos theory and the work of Stephen Hawking and Einstein. Yellow is represented by approximately 1% of the world's population.

8. Turquoise: Individuals of this meme focus on global holism, spiritual connectivity, and meaningful work. They are able to see and honor many perspectives—including first- tier memes. Turquoise focuses on group empowerment and works with collective intelligence to solve global problems while honoring individuality. Co-creative practices and the work of Ken Wilbur, Don Beck, Barbara Marx Hubbard, Jean Houston, and David Bohm exemplify this meme. Turquoise is represented by approximately 1% of the world population.

The goal of what Beck and Cowan call "spiral wizards" is to relate to people, situations, and cultures where they are, or only one-half step ahead of the individuals involved. For example, liberal democracy (Green) is too great a leap for tribal cultures (Red) to understand or appreciate, as was revealed in the wars in Iraq and Afghanistan—when the U.S. led a coalition that was attempting (and failed) to bring western values to tribal people. It was too great a leap.

Spiral wizards honor the truths of all levels and recognize that *all* worldviews are, to some extent, embedded in us, once they have emerged developmentally. Wizards are able to assess a situation and bring the appropriate meme to the forefront to deal with the needs of the moment.

> *If evolution were music, stages of development would be*
> *musical notes, vibrating at a certain frequency.*
> *Human beings would be like strings, capable of*
> *playing many different notes.*
> *The range of notes they can play depends*
> *on the range of tensions they have learned to accommodate.*
>
> DON BECK

> *Never before in human history have we had people operating*
> *from so many different paradigms all living alongside each other.*
> *The same is true for organizations: in the same city...*
> *we can find Red, Orange, and Green Organizations working side by side.*
>
> FREDERIC LALOUX

Quantum Physics and Co-Creation

The book, *Do You Quantum Think?* by Dianne Collins offers a context and an approach to thinking that is invaluable for those who are committed to living co-creative practices and experiencing a more fulfilling life of greater service. The QuantumThink™ system brings together the basics of ancient wisdom and the brilliance of modern physics in 21 distinctions. It supports new thinking that allows practitioners to live fully dimensionally, experience their wholeness, and harness the power of thought to co-create the reality they choose.

In Core Groups, we experience that we are connected energetically to one another through the resonant field of love that we consciously build together. We can experience this invisible field as it expands our personal and collective awareness. We understand this intuitively and can feel energetically the power of co-creative love to build trust, amplify our inner knowing, and bring out the best in each of us.

This is one of many places where spirituality meets science. Physicists explain that quantum entanglement means that particles that appear to be separate are not. When one particle is stimulated, there is an instantaneous exchange of energy and information with all other particles. Everything is connected to everything else at the quantum level. Separation is truly an illusion.

We live in a unified field and are aspects of one whole living entity. What we have known for centuries spiritually, physicists have proven in the past century through science. The field is real; the field connects; the field supports our individual and collective evolution. Quantum physics proves that the universe is holistic and holographic: everything impacts everything else, and the whole is contained in every part.

David Bohm, the great quantum physicist, explained that the underlying reality of these connections at the quantum level is hidden from our view. He called this the *implicate* order, which is enfolded in the background and is invisible. He named the ordinary world that is visible, the *explicate* order; and it is this continuous movement of the enfolding into the unfolding that he named the holo-movement of the universe. There is the "actual world" and the "possible world," and our dreams and visions have existence in the imaginal realm of all possibilities. By focusing our attention and intention on those dreams, we support their unfoldment in the world. We turn the invisible into the visible. Simply by observing, we co-create a new reality. We experience that consciousness is the ultimate reality and the essence of who we are.

The principles of co-creation are manifestations of the implicate order. They are elements of the divine pattern that exists in the invisible realm and can be accessed when we still our minds and turn within. Spirituality meets science in us through the gift of consciousness and our desire to evolve as unique beings in service to the greater good.

The distinctions of quantum thinking add a dimension of understanding that reinforces the practices that we experience when we connect with one another in our Core Groups in a field of love, trust, and safety.

Science is the contemporary language of mysticism.

JOE DISPENZA

We can say that inseparable quantum interconnectedness
of the whole universe is the fundamental reality....
any attempt to assert the independent existence
of a "part" would deny this unbroken wholeness.

DAVID BOHM

Passionate intent combined with unconflicted behavior
changes the structure of the Universe.

JOSEPH CHILTON PEARCE

Starting the Core Group Process™

The circle is the mother of all organizational forms
and the foundation of the earliest human cultures—those with
the deepest connection to the living world in which they were embedded.

RIA BAECK AND HELEN TITCHEN BEETH

Before You Begin

BEFORE CREATING A Core Group, take time to reflect on your purpose and your intent. When you are clear, begin sharing your interest with the friends and the individuals you feel guided to contact. Remember that resonance is the heart of this process, so you will want to invite friends with whom you feel a heart connection.

Forming a Core Group is a bit like courting. Do not expect that your first Core Group will necessarily be your life partners, any more than your first date will be the one you marry! It usually takes a few meetings for a group to "gel" and bond. At the conclusion of this trial time period, the group members can state whether or not this group seems to be the right one for them at this time. The members who choose to remain might create a ceremony to honor their participation.

How many people may attend each gathering? Our experience is that four or five people is the minimum for a Resonant Core Group that is focusing on personal evolution and transformation. Six to ten people is a good size to allow for intimate sharing. You will need to determine the best number for your group and purpose. A Co-creative Core Group that has come together around a shared purpose can be effective with as few as two or three members.

Before your initial meeting, read the Introduction and Sections 1 and 2 of this *Handbook*. Select a facilitator, so that this person can become familiar with the material and experiential exercises before the meeting convenes. Although it's best if the role of facilitator rotates among members of the group, you may find that some people are more adept or natural in this role than others. It's fine to empower those people to fill this role, so long as you acknowledge the equality of all participants and empower others to fill other roles.

The Initial Meetings

---❈---

COMING TOGETHER IN the first session to align around purpose and commitment is vital for the success of the group. Effective gatherings of co-creators have the following characteristics:

- Resonance
- A shared intent and purpose
- Empowerment of each individual member
- A commitment to each other and to the group

At your initial meeting or meetings:

- Agree on your shared purpose
- Align behind a shared intent
- Agree to maintain confidentiality
- Begin to cultivate group resonance
- Align behind your version of The Co-Creator's Agreements

Some examples of shared purpose:

- To support each other as you evolve and deal with transitions in your lives
- To discover and clarify the life purpose of each member of your group
- To develop a particular project or community event
- To model new forms of communication and social cooperation as you bring a vision into manifestation

After reading the introductory material, be sure to begin with Circle 1 of the *Handbook* if your purpose focuses on your personal and collective evolution or your desire to clarify your soul's purpose. If you are drawn to work on a project together, review the first Circles of the *Handbook* and begin with those that feel most relevant to your group. Whether you are creating a Resonant Core Group or a Co-creative Core, you will find that the practices in the first five Circles are always relevant to mastering co-creative processes.

Basic questions that will eventually need to be discussed include:

- When and where will you meet?
- What is the minimum number of weeks or months the group wants to commit to attending?
- How many times may someone miss (other than for being out of town or having a prescheduled commitment) before it's a clear sign that he is choosing not to fully participate?
- Are friends and visitors welcome? [2]

Allow at least three hours for your first meeting. If you are the host, create a safe space—physically and emotionally. Choose an inviting, peaceful environment, free of distractions. Play beautiful background music as people are arriving. Unplug the phone. Ask your family to give you privacy. If you are attending the meeting, arrive on time and leave on time.

Begin with a brief attunement or centering practice. If you wish, use the guided meditation at the end of this Section and also available online as a recording at www.cocreatorshandbook. com. Initial introductions around the circle are important in building resonance and trust. You may want to invite each person to describe their personal passion in life and to share their reason for joining your group.

At one of your first meetings, read the following Co-Creator's Agreements out loud to each other. Take time to discuss them. Agree to lovingly remind each other of these agreements if anyone forgets! *At a future meeting, you may want to re-create or add to these Agreements*, so that they are more personal, relevant, and meaningful for your group. It is important that you make them your own—which might mean rewriting so that they are expressed in language that speaks to your circle. (There is an exercise in Circle 2 called Working with the Co-Creator's Agreements.)

---

2 Probably the most difficult decision to make is what to do with out-of-town visitors or interested friends and family. It seems like a contradiction to exclude anyone when a fundamental purpose of the group is to experience unity; however, deep bonding, trust, and sharing is difficult to achieve if the group is continually changing. Most groups have experienced that it's best to close the circle to others after the third session and create a special session at the completion of the *Handbook* to include those who have expressed interest. Other groups keep several places available for newcomers at each meeting as a way to broaden the opportunities for others. If you decide to admit new members, it is suggested that you do selected processes from Circles 1, 2, and 3 to help bring the group quickly into resonance.

You will notice that the focus of these Agreements is on the individual. You might want to add some agreements that come from the perspective of the group. (For example, the first agreement could be: Our intent is to be fully present with one another.)

The Co-Creator's Agreements

Be Mindful

My INTENT IS to be myself, to be authentic, and to be fully present.

Realize Potential

My commitment is to realize my full potential and support others in doing the same.

Follow My Guidance

I agree to attune with Spirit and follow the calling of my soul on behalf of the well-being of the whole.

Communicate with Integrity

I agree to tell my truth with compassion for myself and others.

Act with Integrity

I agree to keep my agreements and will do my best to follow my heart in making commitments.

Deep Listening

I agree to listen respectfully to the communication of others and tune into their deepest meaning.

Spirit of Curiosity

I engage with others in a spirit of open-heartedness and open-minded curiosity, releasing any personal agenda or positionality that might create separation with another.

Honor One Another

I agree to honor each person's process, acknowledging that everyone—including myself—is making the best possible choice or decision we are capable of in that moment.

Appreciate Contributions

I agree to acknowledge others for their contributions to the whole.

Honor Our Differences

I agree to come from a sense of cooperation and caring in my interactions with others and from an understanding that objectives are often the same, even though methods for achieving them may differ. I honor the diversity of all life.

Take Responsibility

I agree to take responsibility for my creations, my reactions, my experience and my relationships.

Maintain Resonance

I agree to take the time to establish rapport and then to re-connect with anyone with whom I feel out of harmony as soon as it may be appropriate.

Resolve Problems Constructively

I agree to take problems, complaints, and upsets to the person(s) with whom I can resolve them, at the earliest opportunity. I agree not to criticize or complain to someone who cannot do something about my complaint, and I will redirect others to do the same.

Go for Excellence

I agree to support others and to be supported in participating at the highest level of excellence.

Learn from Experience

I agree to do my best to learn from my experience.

Accept Imperfections

I intend to embrace and accept the imperfections of myself and others.

Be a Leader

I agree to foster an environment of genuine collaboration in which all people, including myself, feel empowered to express our individual and collective potential.

Service to Others

I am willing to open my heart, still my mind, and be in compassionate service to all life.

Re-evaluate my Commitment

I agree to choose and re-choose to participate in this Core Group. It's my choice.

Lighten UP!

I agree to create joy in my relationships, my work, and my life.

These Agreements have been adapted from the Geneva Group Agreements, Boulder, CO.

Suggested Meeting Format

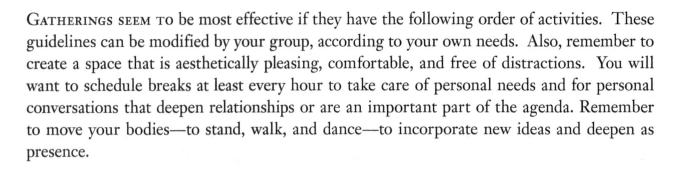

GATHERINGS SEEM TO be most effective if they have the following order of activities. These guidelines can be modified by your group, according to your own needs. Also, remember to create a space that is aesthetically pleasing, comfortable, and free of distractions. You will want to schedule breaks at least every hour to take care of personal needs and for personal conversations that deepen relationships or are an important part of the agenda. Remember to move your bodies—to stand, walk, and dance—to incorporate new ideas and deepen as presence.

    A. Centering or Attunement
    B. Check-in
    C. The purpose of the gathering
    D. Closing

A. Centering or Attunement

Beginning a gathering with some form of centering is an important part of bringing your group together in resonance. The purpose of centering is to reaffirm your connection to Source and with each other and to be fully present. Only by going beyond distractions and accessing Self can you tap into the unlimited resources of Spirit.

Open your session with the guided meditation that is given—or create your own attunement process. (Many recorded meditations are available at www.cocreatorshandbook.com.)

It is helpful to quiet the mind, releasing rambling thoughts, by focusing on the breath and visualizing the body as a clear channel for light energy. The ultimate goal of a co-creator is to be centered at all times in all situations. This occurs naturally as presence takes dominion over personality.

B. Check-in

The check-in is another important activity that brings your group into resonance. The purpose is to share with each other where you are physically, emotionally, mentally, and spiritually at that particular moment in time. If just one person is not in alignment, the group will not attain its full power and potential. An individual check-in may consist of a word or phrase. This is a time for total honesty about what is true for you so that you can be fully present and resonant in the group.

The check-in may include some details about what has brought you to where you are at this particular moment; the purpose is not to tell stories. Generally, it is helpful to limit check-ins to two minutes or less.

Discussions in Core Groups are different from ordinary social talk. The ultimate purpose is to allow the Essential Self to speak. Complaints and negative statements break the group resonance and lower the frequency of the circle, as do gossip and "small talk." Speak and listen from your heart.

After check-ins, make brief announcements and deal with logistics so that the flow of the meeting is not broken by dealing with the necessary details. If you have not already selected who will play the key roles, you can do that at this time. (Key Roles are discussed on the next page.) Read aloud one or more of The Co-Creator's Agreements, if you wish.

If someone in the group is feeling out of resonance with another member, this might be an opportunity to set a date to resolve that issue—either privately or with the group.

C. The Purpose of the Gathering

Having attuned and checked-in, you're ready to attend to the purpose that is bringing you together. Read the introduction to the relevant Circle or any other inspired writing that is related to the co-creative practice you are working with at this meeting. Experience one of the exercises or discuss some of the material in the chapter.

The main content of your meeting may include physical or mental exercises, processes, visualizations, or discussions to develop aspects of the co-creative model or to focus on a particular project or objective. The purpose of the gathering might also be to celebrate and play or to conduct a ceremony.

D. The Closing

The purpose of the closing is to reaffirm your connections and to hold and maintain the resonant field of your group until you come together again. *Remember that everything shared in your Core Group is confidential. Do not discuss the details of member's lives outside the group.*

Key Roles

In advance of each gathering—or at the beginning of each meeting—it is helpful to designate which group members will take responsibility for the key roles. This provides a structure that helps to actualize your purpose and intent. At first, it may feel important to rotate these roles so that each person is empowered and has the opportunity to practice all aspects of being a co-creator. Very quickly, each person will find the natural place to share her gifts with the group. *The guiding principles of the Core Group Process™ are that the leadership rotates, responsibility is shared, and Spirit is the ultimate authority!*

A. The Facilitator

The group gives the facilitator the temporary authority to lead, with the full understanding that everyone is a leader and each person is a full participant in the process. In time, you will discover who the natural facilitators are in your group. It is important to remember that, whenever possible, the facilitator is also a full participant in the various exercises of each Circle.

B. The Timekeeper

The timekeeper's responsibility is to stay connected to the dimension of time so that the others can let go of time concerns. Much of what occurs in Core Groups is "out of time" but third-dimensional-world concerns may require you to agree on time parameters. The time-keeper may time check-ins or let you know when you need to complete a process and move on.

C. The Nurturer / Heart-keeper

The nurturer provides for the physical support of the gathering and creates an environment that is comfortable, quiet, peaceful, and free of distractions. This person also gently reminds everyone when the love energy vital to resonance is blocked or withdrawn. Every person in the group has the responsibility to do their part to maintain the resonance, but in the excitement of the moment, it's easy to move from heart to head and feel separate from one another. The heart-keeper reminds the group to bring themselves back to center, to keep the love flowing, and to pay attention to the needs of their bodies. *Only a resonant group can access higher mind and collective wisdom and experience co-creation!*

D. The Scribe

The scribe keeps track of what happened, the alignment that was reached, the agreements that were made, and the significant information that was shared. Depending on the purpose of the meeting, a scribe may or may not be necessary. Typically, Resonating Core Groups do not have scribes and Co-creative Core Groups do.

The Council Process: Using a Talking Stick

To facilitate heartfelt uninterrupted discussions during a meeting or gathering, you many choose to use the model of the Native American "talking stick" to allow each person to fully share in the group. The purpose of this practice is to remind you that all words that are spoken are sacred. Any object, such as a stone or small sacred object can serve as the talking piece.

BASIC GUIDELINES FOR COUNCIL INCLUDE:

- The person who is holding the talking piece has the right to speak without interruption. He is invited to "speak leanly" in a focused way and from the heart.
- Everyone listens carefully, holding loving presence.
- All participants agree to maintain confidentiality.
- When each person is finished speaking, he says, "I am complete."
- When another person chooses to speak, he accepts the sacred object from the last speaker or takes it from the center of the circle.
- The speaker takes a brief moment to center himself and speaks directly from Essence with clarity and simplicity, as best he is able.
- Expressing in silence is always an honorable contribution. No one is ever forced to speak.

Differentiation

It usually takes a few meetings for a group to come into coherence and to bond with one another. At the conclusion of this trial time period, the group members can state whether or not this group seems to be the right one for them at this time. The members who chose to remain might create a ceremony to indicate that the group is an entity to which they are a member.

If, on the other hand, a member finds that the group is no longer meeting his needs—or that his schedule has changed—he will want to differentiate. Society does not give us good models for departing gracefully with good feelings. Many times in our culture, someone separates from a group by:

- Silently withdrawing from active participation
- Fading away without a complete communication to all group members
- Making the group "wrong" so that the person feels that he has a legitimate reason for leaving (This may or may not be verbalized to others.)

When it is time for someone to leave the group, it is useful to frame this process as "differentiation," rather than separation. Differentiation is a movement into right relationship based on your soul's purpose and inner guidance, rather than a negative move. It continues to acknowledge your connection to everyone and to all life. It is handled in a spirit of love and support. You may want to conduct a ceremony to mark a member's departure from the group.

It is *strongly* suggested that a group never decide to disband unless all members are present. Failure to do this often leads to lingering hurt feelings between the group members who were not present.

You will find additional information about the differentiation process in Circle 6: Expressing Your Soul's Purpose.

A Sample Guided Meditation

NOTE: YOU CAN go to www.cocreatorshandbook.com and listen to the recording of this meditation.

Play soft heartfelt music in the background, if you wish. The facilitator reads slowly:

Gently close your eyes and invite your mind to release any thoughts or plans . . . Take several deep breaths and feel your body relaxing.

(Pause)

As you take another breath and then slowly release it, feel a glow emanating from your heart. . . this is the life force, the Impulse of Creation, flowing through your body . . . Take a moment to experience this mystery of divine intelligence animating matter.

(Pause)

Now imagine you are standing in a peaceful place in nature . . . Be aware of the serenity of the scene before you.

(Pause)

After a moment you notice a light in the distance . . . The light moves and dances in the wind . . and you realize that this light is radiating from a small group of people.

(Pause)

Feel a quickening of your Spirit, a knowing that these beings are like you in so many ways . . . You sense that you are on a similar path . . . You feel drawn to them and you move in their direction. As you draw closer, you may begin to recognize the faces of people you know and respect.

(Pause)

Silently join hands and feel your energy blending with theirs. . . A feeling of connection and rapport envelopes you as you reflect on the blessing of friendship.

(Pause)

Gradually you begin swaying and moving in a beautiful dance . . . reflecting the rhythm of the universe. . . You feel a sense of trust with each person in the circle . . . You know in your heart that anything you do or say would be understood and accepted. You feel safe here . . . safe, protected, and held.

(Pause)

You may feel an inner sense of partnership and promise. . . a knowing that what awaits is a new beginning, the mysterious emergence of something new coming into your life. . . You are filled with a sense of anticipation and the vision of a new creation . . . new possibilities.

(Pause)

Now take a deep breath into your heart and sense yourself back in this time and space . . . Be aware of the life force moving within you, bringing vitality to every cell of your body . . . presence expressing through physical form . . . When you are ready, open your eyes, and consciously connect with the others in your circle.

Experiencing
the Circles of Co-Creation

*This section of the book is unique and should be
approached differently from all other sections.
It is to be <u>experienced</u>, rather than read.*

CIRCLE 1

Awakening the Co-Creative Self

Inside every human is a God in embryo.
It has only one desire … it wants to be born.

KAHLIL GIBRAN

There is no self to be dissolved.
There is only the notion of self to be transcended.

THICH NHAT HANH

You are the One you are seeking, pretending to be a seeker.

THE WAY OF MASTERY

When you make the two one;
And when you make the inside like the outside
And the outside like the inside;
And when you make the above as the below;
When you make the male and the female into a single one,
So that the male will not be male and the female not be female—
Then shall you enter the Kingdom.

THE GOSPEL OF THOMAS

Humanity stands at the threshold of a new dawning.
The challenges and imperatives of our time are calling forth
greater creativity and awakening millions of people
to their true nature and potential.

Like butterflies emerging from the cocoon,
we are awakening as Whole Beings,
tapping into the essence of our nature,
capable of co-creating with the divine intelligence of Spirit.

One day we meet someone, or read a book, or have an experience
and something shifts within. An awakening occurs.
We come home to our Self.

Our soul is sparked and we know we must follow inner guidance
and the promptings of our heart.

Eventually, when this Self is activated,
we stand poised as presence to give our gifts, share our love,
and fully experience the grandeur of our beings.

We are reborn, and we rejoice in this shift in identity.
We realize that we are no thing at all. We are pure consciousness,
the Impulse of Creation expressing in unique form as us.

Awakening the Co-Creative Self

EACH OF US is on a hero or heroine's journey. We are coded with our spiritual possibility and are mysteriously moved from within to evolve and awaken to our true nature. The deep innate longing to express our full potential pulls us forward; and, at the same time, personal challenges drive us to search for satisfying alternatives to old habits, tendencies, and ways of thinking that are not working.

As we begin the process of waking up to our true identity, we step out of our comfort zone and face the inner demons and outer challenges of our daily lives. Over time, we find allies along the way: those who stand by our side and assist us in moving forward. The prize we seek, the pot of gold at the end of the rainbow, is the experience of coming home to our Self, ready and desirous to give our gifts to the world as full co-creators.

At some point, we experience that we are more than our limited thoughts, emotions, and physical bodies. We discover that at the center of our being there is a life force or higher power animating all that we are and do. In a state of expanded awareness, we experience a broader sense of Self; and when we do, we feel fulfilled and at home in our own being. The Self we come home to is not a person or a place. It is the vast space in which everything happens. It is awareness, the supreme reality—the Impulse of Creation itself, operating through us, as us.

This Self has many names: the Essential Self, the Beloved, the Authentic Self, the soul, loving awareness, or simply presence. By whatever name, the experience of accessing our true nature feels normal and liberating. It happens from the inside out. An external crisis may serve as motivation, but the real work occurs within. Something awakens or emerges and we are new.

We finally become free of at least most of our personal conditioning and are not reactivated by the projections of others and the rules of our society. We begin to relate *to* the mind, rather than *from* the mind. Our identity shifts: our personality becomes a vehicle for the expression of presence in the world, rather than an obstacle. We don't lose our ego; we simply stop identifying with it and start observing its tendencies. Over time, we move internally from one state of being to a more expansive stage, stabilizing at a higher frequency in tune with the Divine. We feel the alignment of all aspects of our being: body, personality self, Authentic Self, and—as we give expression to our true calling—our co-creative Self. We feel at one with the One that appears as many.

We have always been and will always be this presence. As we move from self-centered consciousness to whole-centered consciousness, we recognize that we are not in charge. We release struggle, effort, and the desire to control. We fall into the arms of the Beloved and relax. Gradually, Essence or presence transcends and includes the ego, honoring the personality self as a vehicle for true Self expression.

We know intuitively that an invisible intelligence is orchestrating a divine dance. As we surrender to this guiding source, we begin to trust, let go, and accept "what is." This takes a leap of faith and the willingness to do the personal work that is required: to face and move through the faults, fears, and illusions of our egoic, separate selves. We know that our task is to wake up to our true identity and to allow our healing to be felt energetically and not simply conceptually. When we are ready, we put this purpose first.

Through conscious intent, vigilance, and practice, we learn to turn to our inner knowing. We may get ideas from others, but we take these ideas to the quiet place within and let all issues be decided here. As the process unfolds, we gradually become neutral observers, watching life unfold in our presence. Our "doing" flows effortlessly from our being. We are humbled and awed by the great mystery, ready to take our next turn on the evolutionary spiral as Whole Beings, honored to have life live its dance through us, as us. We give up the desire to be special and experience that we are Divine.

The activities of this chapter are primarily individual, ongoing daily practices that are designed to keep us centered and aware as loving presence. We have learned that the road to integrating our personality self with our invisible Essence can be bumpy and unpredictable. It requires commitment and support, particularly when we are experiencing fear, doubt, or any other emotional contraction. *This step of coming home to Self is critical to discovering our purpose and joining cooperatively with others.* As we dream our dreams and tune into the needs of the whole, the spirit of creation molds energy and potential into matter, magnetizing the perfect people and activities that are needed for our soul's evolution at any given time.

These practices prepare us to eventually join with others who are ready to co-create. We experience that linking with partners, heart to heart, center to center, lifts our energy frequency and amplifies our creative expression. An inner shift occurs as we tap into the power of creation. Gradually, we are able to detach from the oscillating circumstances of our lives and become impartial observers . . . celebrating what is, as it is . . . "in the world but not of it."

The next stage of evolution is to live as Essence, to act from this place of deep trust and knowing—to become a co-creator: consciously aligning in resonance with others and with the evolutionary impulse which leads to higher consciousness, greater coherence, and freedom. Our hero's or heroine's journey is an internal movement from identification with the personality self to the experience of communion with all that is—as loving awareness.

Note: The exercises in this Chapter will take more than one meeting to complete. We encourage you to read the book *Emergence: The Shift from Ego to Essence* by Barbara Marx Hubbard, in conjunction with experiencing these exercises.

Guided Meditation: Becoming Centered

The facilitator slowly reads this aloud, remembering to pause between phrases. You may want to play soft beautiful music in the background. If you prefer, you can play the recording of this meditation that is available online at www.cocreatorshandbook.com.

Gently close your eyes. Create an aura of silence around you. As best you are able, release any sense of age or gender . . . any identity with roles or responsibilities.

(Pause)

Feel your connection to the Earth and invite your body to relax . . . Focus your awareness on your feet and feel the life force moving through your feet . . . Now place your attention on your legs, inviting them to release any tension, any stress . . . Now, let that feeling of total, complete relaxation move into your upper extremities . . . your abdomen . . . and your back . . . your arms and your hands. Shrug or shake out your shoulders so that they feel completely free of tension. Breathe deeply . . . and feel the breath relaxing your neck . . . jaw . . . eyes . . . your scalp.

(Pause)

Feel at peace as you continue to concentrate on your breath . . . Breathing deeply and naturally, feeling the life force move throughout your physical form.

(Pause)

And with your next breath . . . imagine the Earth's strength coming into every cell of your body. Imagine the love and wisdom of Spirit flowing through the crown of your head . . . connecting to and fusing with the energy of the Earth in your heart.

(Pause)

Now place your attention on your heart . . . Allow the warmth of your love for nature, for the Divine, and for life itself to permeate your being . . . Feel the utter peace, the joy of that love. Imagine each breath bringing golden light into your heart . . . Feel the alchemical process of transmutation occurring in your body now . . . warm currents of electrical impulse moving in every cell . . . bringing release and regeneration . . . flooding your physical form and your awareness . . . Feel the energy of love in every cell now, animating and enlivening your entire body.

(Pause)

Feel the spaciousness of your Essential Self as peace and freedom.

(Pause)

Now, slowly bring your awareness back to this present moment . . . slowly moving your hands and feet. When you feel ready, open your eyes and slowly look around the room . . . Make eye contact with each person in this circle . . . Self connecting with Self . . . presence meeting presence.

Process: Introducing One Another

To get to know each other better, pair off and prepare to introduce each other to your group. In each pair, you can share deep insights about yourself with your partner. Allow about five minutes for each person. Then, when the group comes back together, you can introduce your partner. After the introductions to the group, the person being introduced can add to, or clarify, what was said.

Process: Distinguishing between Presence and Personality

The following exercise has many parts. Make sure you have at least 90 minutes to complete all parts of the process in one meeting. Otherwise, you could progress to the section in this chapter on Inner Listening and cover this material in your next meeting.

The list below distinguishes the characteristics of the Essential Self, or presence, and the local personality self, living in the world of duality.

1. Discuss this in your group and co-create any additions or changes.

PRESENCE OR ESSENTIAL SELF	PERSONALITY OR LOCAL SELVES
Oneness; feels connection	Experiences separation
Detached witness	Attached and involved
Identifies with pure awareness	Identifies with the body, thoughts, and emotions
Expansion; no limitation	Contraction; a sense of lack
Flow; ease and grace	Rigidity; effort
Embodied knowing	Thinking
Intimacy; nothing to hide	Defensiveness; protecting self image
Acceptance of what is	Manipulation; assertion of personal will
Allowing; trusting; welcoming	Resisting; judging
Present; in the moment	Future or past oriented
Being love	Looking for love

Authentic	Saving face; wearing a mask
Acknowledges mistakes; humble	Blames; scapegoats; projects on others
Transpersonal	Personalizes the impersonal
Inner peace	Fear; anxiety
Spontaneous	Strategic
Free	May want to control or dominate
Imperishable and eternal	Mortal and temporal

2. Make a list of aspects of your local personality self (for example, the critic, the worrier, the victim, the blamer, etc.)

Local selves are, in reality, thoughts in your mind! For example, victim consciousness, jealousy, regret, and resentment come from the past; worry, anxiety, and concern are negative projections onto the future. Love, peace, and a deep sense of well-being—aspects of the Essential Self— live only in the moment and are accessed by being fully present! At another time you may want to discuss this in your group and tap into your personal experience to see if it's true for you!

3. Next, with heartfelt music playing in the background, take a few minutes to write a detailed description of your Essential Self. Select all the qualities that you most admire.

4. The facilitator slowly reads the following, with soft music playing in the background. Be sure to pause between phrases to allow the members of your group to fully experience the meditation.

Guided Meditation: Embracing Local Selves

The facilitator slowly reads this aloud, remembering to pause between phrases. If you prefer, you can play the recording of this meditation, available online at www.cocreatorshandbook.com.

Gently close your eyes and allow your body to relax fully . . . Take a few full breaths and place your awareness on your Essence, the timeless aspect of your being . . . As Essence, call forth those local selves that live most strongly within you . . . Reflect for a moment on these facets of your personality.

(Pause)

Now bring one of these separate, local selves into awareness . . . Notice the behavior, the body posture, the facial expression . . . What is this separate self doing? . . . How is it feeling?

(Pause)

Step forward as your Essential Self and invite this local self to come into your arms . . . Open your heart to this quality . . . Feel compassion and empathy for the struggle it experiences . . . Feel this local self taking in your love and energy and responding by dropping its need to act up for attention . . . How does it want to be honored? Appreciate the way in which this aspect of your personality has served your growth . . . Feel the flow of love between presence and personality . . .back and forth . . . healing any judgment or sense of separation that might have existed here . . . Now, tenderly feel this local self coming into wholeness as Essence continues to embrace it with love.

(Pause)

Bring into awareness a different local self . . . Notice the behavior, the body posture, the facial expression . . . What is this local self doing?. . . How is it feeling?. . . Once again, step forward as Essence and invite this local self to come into your arms . . . acknowledge this quality . . . feel compassion and empathy for the struggle it experiences. Say anything you need to say to the local self in gratitude for its gift in your life. Listen for any response. Again, feel this local self taking in your love and energy . . . dissolving the illusion of separation.

(Pause)

Now imagine that all other aspects of your personality are like your children . . . and as a compassionate parent, bring them into a loving embrace . . . With a sense of gratitude for all the ways in which they have served you, feel this integration occurring at a cellular level . . . no aspect of yourself is left behind.

(Pause)

Envision the qualities of the Essential Self woven into a beautiful invisible cloak that you slip on and can wear all day, every day . . . Feel these qualities emanating from you and embracing you . . . Claim your identity as the Self as you bring your ideal nature into reality.

(Pause)

Reflect on how you and others would benefit by living as the Self in the world.

(Pause)

Now, take a few deep breaths and, when you're ready, slowly open your eyes and bring your awareness back into the room.

Take a few minutes to write down your insights and share them with the other members of your group.

This might be a good time to take a break or complete this session. You may want to put on some music and move your bodies before sharing a closing exercise or proceeding to the next exercise.

Practicing Self-Awareness

It appears that self-reflective humans are pre-programmed to "know thyself." At some point in our lives, most conscious people ask themselves: "Who am I?" "Where am I going?" "Why am I here?"

The practice of Self-awareness or mindfulness can be done anywhere and anytime. It is to be aware of one's present moment experience—mentally, emotionally, and physically. It means noticing what is occurring externally in one's environment and internally in the body/mind. In addition, it means being aware of what meaning we give to our experiences. Ultimately, as we awaken, we begin to notice our responses without being reactivated—without trying to change or resist any experience.

Tips for Inner Listening

READ ALOUD AND discuss the following guidelines. In the next exercise, you will have an opportunity to experience this foundational co-creative practice.

- To practice inner listening, sit in a peaceful, undisturbed environment that supports you in centering yourself. Close your eyes, relax your posture, and breathe deeply.
- Quiet your mind, emotions, and body. Be aware of them, but look beyond them to the calm and loving space of the Self.
- Pose a question and open up to inner knowing without investment or attachment to what you experience. Often the first response is the clearest.
- Be cautious of interpretations and trying to figure things out. The truth is simple. Look to the energy of the response, in addition to the content of the response, as a more reliable guideline.
- Listen with assurance, knowing that you are being directed even when you are unaware. Be in full observation of everything that is occurring in your experience.
- Accept without judgment whatever you hear, see, or sense. If you desire more clarity or assurance, ask for it. Then act on the guidance you receive.
- If in doubt, keep listening. You will always know the truth when it comes to you and brings insight and understanding to your world. Perhaps, an immediate response may not be timely or a "non-response" may be important in the moment.
- Go within often and make it a normal part of your life—as though it were a "waking meditation." Avoid "foxhole praying" or only connecting in emergencies.
- Ask for an opening "for the highest good" in any area of your life needing assistance. Let go of expectations. Just be open and ready to receive and learn.
- Envision and affirm answers being given and demonstrated to you.
- Use art, creative writing, visualization, dance, music, being in nature, and other creative forms to assist in accessing inspired insights.

Guided Process: Inner Listening

The facilitator slowly reads this aloud, remembering to pause between phrases.

Take a few full breaths into your heart and invite your body to relax.

(Pause)

Begin to formulate a question that is meaningful to you at this time in your life.

(Pause)

If a question does not come, ask yourself: What do I need to do to bring my life into greater balance?

(Pause)

Allow an answer to emerge . . . It may come as intuition or deep knowing, or as a feeling or body sensation . . . You may even hear words.

(Pause)

If nothing comes, just relax and take another few deep breaths.

(Pause)

In a few minutes, open your eyes and record any inspirations, insights, or feelings that have arisen for you.

When everyone is ready, share your experiences with one another.

Guided Meditation: The Heart Meditation

For millennia, people in the Eastern world have followed a practice called Tonglen. It was described in the first century by the Tibetan Heart master Atisha. He called it "giving and taking on the breath." The following practice can be used privately, with a partner, or with your entire Core Group to open your hearts more fully.

The facilitator slowly reads this aloud, remembering to pause between phrases. You may want to play soft beautiful music in the background. If you prefer, you can play the recording of this meditation—available online at www.cocreatorshandbook.com.

Sit comfortably and close your eyes . . . Take a few deep breaths and relax your body.

(Pause)

Focus your awareness on the middle of your chest, the heart center . . . You might imagine that you are fanning the flames of the heart with each in-breath . . . Feel the flame spreading throughout your body on the out-breath.

(Pause)

Visualize your heart center as a window into the vastness that is your true nature . . . From this place of limitlessness, look out at the world of form . . . Now imagine breathing form back in through the window of the heart . . . Breathe in form and breathe out formlessness, emptiness . . . Radiate presence and love with every exhalation.

(Pause)

Notice any thoughts and breathe them in through the window of the heart . . . Once again, breathe in form and breathe out formlessness . . . Radiate silence that is empty of thought.

(Pause)

Now notice any emotions and breathe them in through the window of the heart . . . Take all the time you need to breathe in emotions and breathe out emptiness.

(Pause for 1 - 2 minutes)

Now continue to do the same with any physical sensations you may be feeling . . . Breathe in any sensations you are feeling and breathe out warmth, love, and stillness.

(Pause for 1 - 2 minutes)

Continue to absorb with the in-breath . . . and radiate with the out-breath . . . Make no distinction between thoughts, emotions, and physical sensations . . . Continue with this practice until it becomes as natural as breathing.

(Pause)

Slowly open your eyes and continue to radiate love and silence.

Process: Practicing the Heart Meditation with a Partner

Pair up with another member of your Core Group. Face one another and for five minutes practice breathing in form and breathing out formlessness. Envision the two of you connecting as one, releasing all sense of boundaries and distinctions that arise in the world of form. You may choose to use the Heart Meditation on a regular basis at future meetings. As you progress in this process, you can use it to send healing energies to specific individuals, situations, or to the Earth.

Process: Connecting Self to Self

The purpose of this first exercise is to support the shift in identity from ego to Essence as you acknowledge and reinforce timeless qualities of presence. The timekeeper can prompt you when to begin and signal you to stop and reverse roles, when that is appropriate. If you wish, you may each take additional turns to deepen the experience. Allow 30 to 40 minutes for this process.

- Pair up and sit facing each other. Look deeply into each other's eyes and connect heart to heart. Practice the heart meditation for a few minutes.

Partner A begins by asking Partner B: "Who are you?" Speaking as Essence, Partner B responds: "I am _____." Partner A says, "Thank you." and then asks again, "Who are you?" This sequence continues for two or three minutes, allowing Partner B to respond with "I am _____" each time. Do not consciously "think" about it, just say whatever comes to you. When you are ready, reverse roles and repeat the process.

- In this second exercise, you are guided to experience yourself as pure awareness.

Facing your partner, spend a few minutes centering in the Heart Meditation. When you feel ready, Partner A says, "Tell me about that which is looking." Partner B responds spontaneously. Partner A repeats the statement after each response: "Tell me about that which is looking." Continue this process for a few minutes and then reverse roles. Allow at least three minutes for each person each time. When you are complete, sit together in silence. Allow your eyes to meet as you sink deeply into presence, Self meeting Self.

When you have completed the process, acknowledge your partner. Then come together and share in the larger circle.

You are the luminous source out of which brilliance arises.

ARJUNA ARDAGH

*Human beings are not problems waiting to be solved,
but potential waiting to unfold.*

FREDERIC LALOUX

Guided Meditation: Meeting the Beloved

The facilitator slowly reads this aloud, remembering to pause between phrases. You may want to play soft, beautiful music in the background. If you prefer, you can play the recording of this meditation that is available online at www.cocreatorshandbook.com. Allow 30 minutes for this process.

Close your eyes. Take a few deep breaths and invite your body to relax completely.

(Pause)

See yourself in a beautiful, peaceful place in nature . . . Take in the sounds and smells that are present . . . Breathe deeply and let go . . . There is nothing to do . . . Just relax . . . Allow any thoughts that are arising to float by . . . like clouds in the vast blue sky.

(Pause)

Breathe in and out through your heart . . . Breathe in love . . . radiate love . . . Allow the breath to open your heart ever more fully . . . Invite the presence of love to permeate every cell in your body.

(Pause)

Imagine this presence of love bursting forth and taking form in front of you . . . This is the Beloved, your ideal being . . . the aspect of your Self that you have been seeking . . . Take a close look at this Beloved . . . it may be energetic and ethereal or it may be visible to sight. Notice as precisely as possible all aspects of this being as it appears to you.

(Pause)

When you feel safe with this Beloved . . . speak silently to this being . . . Ask any questions . . . express any fears . . . call forth any wisdom . . . Tell the Beloved your needs and aspirations.

(Pause for 1 - 2 minutes)

Now listen to the Beloved . . . Allow this dialogue to continue, as you ask questions and listen to the response of the Beloved.

(Pause for 1 - 2 minutes)

Now become the Beloved . . . See and feel yourself actually merging with the Beloved . . . Look through these eyes . . . feel these feelings . . . Notice how the body feels . . . Be aware of the grandeur and expansiveness of this being . . . Slowly, shift your identity and acknowledge that you are the Beloved . . . That which you have been seeking in the world is who you are . . . You have come home to your Self . . . Feel into the magnificence of your being.

(Pause for 1 - 2 minutes)

Now shift your identity once more . . . Take a few deep breaths and focus on your physical body. Be aware of any emotions that arise . . . Look at the Beloved . . . Continue dialoguing with the Beloved.

(Pause)

Now, once again, shift your identity . . . Become the Beloved and merge into emptiness . . . Feel the love that you are . . . Feel the deep sense of peace that is always present as the Self . . . Notice that you are not male or female . . . You have no age and no gender . . . You are pure awareness . . . all that is . . . whole and complete in your being.

(Pause)

When you're ready, slowly bring your awareness back to the room . . . Look at each person in the circle . . . See the Beloved, the Self, in every member of your group.

When this exercise is complete, some members of the group may want to sit silently, while others may wish to stand and move to the music. Invite journaling to record any insights. Flow with the energy of the group. You may find it desirable to refrain from speaking with one another to honor the depth of the experience.

Create a conscious closing for the meeting.

The ego is an idea of who/what you think you are.

ROBERT WOLFE

When we are in touch with the highest spirit in ourselves,
we too are a Buddha, filled with the Holy Spirit, and we become
very tolerant, very open, very deep, and very understanding.

THICH NHAT HANH

Our highest potential as a species is our ability to achieve
full self-reflective consciousness or "knowing that we know."
Through humanity's awakening, the universe acquires the ability
to look back and reflect back on itself—in wonder, awe, and appreciation.

DUANE ELGIN

Deepening Practices

— ❧ —

The following exercises are to be done on your own.

Centering

A DAILY CENTERING practice can facilitate awakening the Authentic Self. You may find it helpful to stop and breathe deeply when you feel off center. Slow down and allow your personality to be held by your Essence. Practice mindfulness by paying attention to your thoughts, emotions, and body sensations as you go about your daily life. (You may want to experiment with the Buddhist practice of using a bell to call you back to the present moment. For example, you could set the timer on your smart phone to give you an alert every few hours.)

Your Essential Self is the wisest teacher on earth. It knows exactly what is needed at all times. In this respect, it could be called the inner coach. Educate your mind to listen to the inner coach and carry out its orders. If you feel tense, anxious, or disoriented, it means your personality self has taken dominion over Essence. When you feel this way, fully experience the feeling and become a neutral observer. Watch as the feeling dissolves and disappears. *Non-resistance, non-attachment, and non-judgment are keys to true freedom.*

Because there are many practices that you can learn and many paths to experiencing the Self, take the time to explore and find what is right for you.

Co-creators are vigilant and learn to spend more and more time in a centered state. You will know the Essential Self by the feeling of connection with others and with nature—a sense of unity with all. Feeling relaxed, aware, and present in the moment, you experience a sense of mental, emotional, physical, and spiritual balance. You maintain witness consciousness—watching your thoughts and feeling your emotions and body sensations with a sense of detachment. You feel free from the ups and downs of self-centered consciousness.

Observe Your Thoughts, Clarify Your Intent

Whatever gets your attention gets you! What enters the mind repeatedly, shapes the mind. Learn to be a master of your own attention and to be conscious of your stream of thoughts.

Thoughts are impersonal waves of energy, appearing in the space that you are. Let insignificant, unwanted thoughts pass through your awareness, without reacting and without judgment.

Notice when you are operating from your ideas and ideals of how things should be. Can you release "positionality" and embrace what is? Does this process of letting go and observing from a place of neutrality create a sense of greater peace and freedom for you?

The mind cannot differentiate between "reality" and imagination empowered by desire. As you think, so you create. When thoughts challenge you, or difficult decisions arise, do not struggle from an anxious state. Still your mind and ask for guidance. The way will be revealed.

Ask and you will receive. Set aside some time to get in touch with your vision. Think in terms of choices and clarify your dreams and intentions. What kind of life do you want to have? What is your heart yearning to express? Write out the vision of your ideal life and read it frequently. Set your intention and bring your heart's desire into your life by focusing your attention on what you choose. Combine your intention with an elevated emotion, so that your body believes that what you envision has already happened. Creation is a function of focus, not force. Life shows up differently when you shift your focus, clarify your intent, believe in all possibilities, align with your passion, and surrender as infinite presence.

Attention, intention, and heartfelt desire are partners in co-creating the reality you choose.

Keep a Journal

A journal can be a powerful tool for personal growth and transformation. Record your insights and the answers you receive from within. Take time each day, preferably in the early morning while all is quiet, to access your deeper knowing. Pose questions that are relevant to your current situation and write down the guidance that you receive. Create an inner dialogue with the Beloved.

Use your journal to record your journey through this *Handbook*. Write down your dreams. You might want to keep a notepad or voice recorder nearby to capture your insights during the day or night.

Set aside time each day and each week to honor the spiritual dimension of your life. The Self needs sacred time and space to blossom and take dominion.

Embracing Your Shadow

Carl Jung referred to the shadow as the "dark unknown side of the personality." These are the unconscious, instinctive, irrational qualities that we unconsciously project onto others.

By shining the light of awareness on our projections, we move away from feelings of separation, and we move toward greater authenticity—gaining access to aspects of our personal power and creativity that have been unavailable and out of reach. This process requires presence and can be disorienting, as the mind struggles to adapt to new behaviors. As we become aware of these unconscious tendencies, we make progress in overcoming the sense of separation that occurs when we judge others for those qualities that we have not accepted within ourselves.

Aligning Body, Mind, and Spirit

Our circumstances or the events of our lives are a reflection of the alignment or conflict between our body, mind, and Spirit. Life is a mirror of our consciousness. When we are connected as Essence, life seems to flow easily and miraculously. There is a direct link between inspiration and manifestation.

When we are feeling separate and out of touch, we experience struggle and effort. For example, we may feel conflicted inside or have a pain or engage in an argument. By sensing the energy present in each of these occurrences, we can begin to discover what is really going on. It is looking beyond the outward appearances to the consciousness that is causing these things to occur. The purpose of this process is to learn to self-correct when our life circumstances do not reflect our ideals.

Write down the following:

- First, select a circumstance in your life that indicates that something is out of alignment.
- Now, turn to the state of your body, mind, and emotions. How do you feel physically, mentally, and emotionally when you focus on this situation?
- After checking in with all three, what is the consistent thread or message? How are your body, mind, and emotions out of alignment with Spirit?
- Reflect on the choices you are making in your life. How are they affecting you?
- How are your choices affecting those around you?
- Now ask your Self what you can do to bring balance back into your life. Who might you turn to for support and encouragement?

Share your process and insights with your Core Group at your next meeting. The members of your group can bear witness to your intentions and provide encouragement as you make changes in your life.

Taking Responsibility for Your Thoughts, Creations, and Actions

What does it mean to you to take responsibility for everything in your life? Over the next few weeks, contemplate the following: "All relationships and experiences are neutral. I alone place value, give meaning, and make interpretations on these; and in so doing, I create my experience." What would your life be like if you adopted this attitude and took responsibility for your creations and reactions, as suggested in The Co-Creator's Agreements? What would society be like if every person assumed this attitude?

Evolving Consciously

Contemplate the following statement and share any insights with your Core Group when you next meet. Can you relate to what is offered here? Does this ring true for you?

We are crossing a threshold in consciousness at this time. As we place our attention on what is wanting to emerge within us, we begin to feel "new." We notice that old patterns begin to fade and it feels as though our body becomes lighter, more vital, and alive. Our consciousness feels more expansive as we realize that we are embodiments of the divine Impulse of Creation. There is a sense of joy and playfulness as we integrate all aspects of our being and feel whole. By placing our attention on the highest aspect of our being, we can release that which no longer serves and begin to integrate that which is emerging. We can participate consciously in our own evolution as full co-creators, unique and universal fractals of the One.

I Am Not I

by Juan Ramon Jimenez

I am not I.
I am this one
walking beside me whom I do not see,
whom at times I manage to visit,
and whom at other times I forget;
who remains calm and silent while I talk,
and forgives, gently, when I hate,
who walks where I am not,
who will remain standing when I die.

CIRCLE 2

Creating and Maintaining Resonance

When you love, you should not say, "God is in my heart," but rather,
"I am in the heart of God."

KAHLIL GIBRAN

Whenever two or three are gathered in my name, I am there.

JESUS

The attraction of love for love remains irresistible.
For it is the function of love to unite all things unto itself,
and to hold all things together by extending wholeness.

THE COURSE IN MIRACLES

It is only with the heart that one can see clearly,
for what is essential is hidden from the eyes.

ANTOINE DE SAINT EXUPERY

Love allows all things, trusts all things, embraces all things,
and therefore, transcends all things.

THE WAY OF MASTERY

The process of co-creation begins by shifting identity to the Self
and then expressing love as this Self.
This expression of love creates resonance, the invisible
field in which true co-creation occurs.

Resonance blossoms as we love the potential in others
and join in the sacred practices of acceptance,
nonjudgment, trust, and compassion.

The idea of loving one another as ourselves
is the greatest and most obvious precept on earth.
We have all heard it through our religions and ethical systems:
"Do unto others as you would have them do unto you."

Thousands of books have been written, millions of people
give lip service to it. Why would it work now?
Because there is a new condition on Earth,
requiring us to change our behavior if we are to survive.
What was esoteric or impractical in the past is essential now.
The time has come to create a loving world.

In a world where love has been considered soft, weak and ineffectual,
evolution demonstrates that love is the fundamental
unifying and creative force in the universe.

It is powerful, courageous and the most effective
energy available to awaken humanity's potential and "get the job done."
Love is precisely what is needed most now!

Creating and Maintaining Resonance

A NUMBER OF decades ago, British biologist Rupert Sheldrake proposed his concept of morphogenetic fields. According to this hypothesis, all living things are surrounded by non-visible fields that carry information from one generation to the next, thereby making a new behavior easier to learn. Often referred to as the influence of like upon like—this hypothesis suggests that humans themselves are fields of energy, interconnected to all life. As conscious beings we are able to create the kind of energy we transmit. When this energy is imbued with heartfulness and compassion, we call it resonance, the frequency of love.

Resonance lies at the heart of co-creative practices. Retaining equanimity is not always easy. Shifting from the dominator to the partnership model and maintaining an open heart can be a challenge. Co-creative practices can be disruptive and a bit messy. We may be breaking decades of conditioning as an individual and millennia of behavior as a species. Misunderstandings and confusion can be part of the journey of building a new world. It is, however, the way we are choosing to birth and nurture a satisfying life and a compassionate society.

Resonance is born in a field of love, trust, unconditional acceptance, and mutual support and flowers in "safe spaces." It disappears in the face of judgment, criticism, tension, or animosity. It begins with self-love and the unconditional love that is freely given by Spirit. Accepting this love is accepting that one is blessed and worthy of such love; *that one is, in fact, love.* It does not depend on other people; it does not depend on what we do, or on our daily successes and failures. If we judge or condemn ourselves, we are denying the worth of the Divine Impulse and the creation of which we are a part.

Resonance comes from intention, attention, telling the truth, and connecting with one another center to center. Practices such as meditation, yoga, prayer, chanting, song, dance, silence, mindful speech, and conscious movement allow us to attune to higher vibrational frequencies. When we are centered, experiencing ourselves as present awareness, we are in resonance with all that is—and we attract resonance into our lives.

As we believe in our hearts, so it is done. When we connect with others heart to heart, the universal Force of Creation works through us to guide us to our perfect place of service.

When we align our energies in this way, an invisible field of union, oneness, and creativity is born. It brings our aligned energies into coherence. This is the resonant field—the natural home of the Essential Self. We learn to cultivate this energy consciously until it becomes a natural way of being. We intensify our practice in our small groups, and in so doing, we release the highest potential in each member of our circle.

When the love field is sustained, we feel lighter. Our bodies feel less dense as we move to a higher energy frequency. Emotional and physical healing can occur spontaneously as love opens the cells of our bodies, releasing the contractions of anxiety and fear that create disease. Boundaries dissolve. The Essential Self is magnetized into the light of day by the field of love and eventually takes dominion. A vibrating frequency, a harmonic, blends our energies into a common chord and a unified field. We are filled with love and joy.

In our groups, we practice loving our neighbors as ourselves and each other as co-creators. If we love ourselves as aspects of divine intelligence, we can easily love another in the same way. Loving our own gifts, we can appreciate the gifts that others have to offer. Joyfully, we join together for the conscious evolution of ourselves in an accepting world. We experience that cultivating peace and harmony within is a gift to ourselves and to humanity.

When we connect with others at the heart, we take a quantum leap beyond the capacities of individuals alone. Social synergy results, creating a whole that is greater than and different from the sum of its parts. We experience total alignment and a jump in consciousness, freedom, and creativity. We experience that all is one.

Maintaining group resonance is a delicate act of orchestration requiring sensitivity, trust, and the highest integrity. It cannot be forced, but it can be cultivated as an act of both personal and collective practice and will. A successful Core Group is a sacred space that embraces diversity, brings forth individuality, and creates unparalleled possibility for all participants. As such, it is to be honored, nurtured, and graced with the commitment of each member.

Basic Principles to Establish Resonance

Attention: Place your attention on your heart; feel the love that you are.
Attraction: Be aware of your natural affinity for all life: Essence attracted to Essence.

Connection: Experience infinite presence as the One appearing as many.

Intention: Set an intention to experience resonance in every aspect of your life.

Relaxation: Release and trust in the creative process and the transformative power of love.

Please note that the exercises in this Circle will take more than one meeting to complete. Remember to take breaks and to move your body. Shifts in awareness naturally become integrated into the body when we are present in the moment.

Guided Meditation: Creating Resonance

The facilitator slowly reads this aloud, remembering to pause between phrases. You may want to play soft beautiful music in the background. If you prefer, you can play the recording of this meditation—available online at www.cocreatorshandbook.com.

Invite the group to get comfortable, close their eyes, and relax.

Sit with your spine erect . . . and take some deep breaths.

(Pause)

With each exhalation, let any tension and thoughts float away with that breath.

(Pause)

With each inhalation, imagine the breath being drawn into every cell of your body. . . renewing and revitalizing every organ and tissue.

(Pause)

Now, let your breath concentrate in your heart . . . With each inhalation, feel a warmth growing in your heart center . . . like a small flame, glowing like an ember.

(Pause)

As you breathe deeply, that flame grows and sends radiant warmth throughout your body.

(Pause)

Each cell of your body responds as if being bathed in sunlight . . . All your cells begin to vibrate at the same frequency.

(Pause)

Each cell radiates light back to your heart, like waves crossing the ocean . . . Flowing to and from the heart— like a great central sun bathing all life with light.

(Pause)

The golden light in your heart grows even brighter as this energy flows back and forth until you feel your whole body beginning to glow.

(Pause)

Now, let a thread of this light gently float out of your heart toward the center of the circle . . . When it gets to the center, let the thread collect into a little golden ball as it mingles and dances with the other threads being extended from everyone in the room.

(Pause)

Notice how the different energies seem naturally to blend into a larger ball of golden light.

(Pause)

From this enormous ball of light, imagine two shafts of light venturing out: one into the Earth and the other toward the stars . . . Notice how the Earth's energy and the radiance from the stars easily flow into this connected ball of golden energy.

(Pause)

And so it is in truth . . . We are all connected to the Source . . . and to one another always . . . in our hearts.

(Pause)

As we share with each other, let us keep the awareness of this connection present. Let us be aware that when another is speaking, it is just another aspect of our Self which is speaking.

(Pause)

Now, slowly, taking whatever time you need, begin to become aware of your body again . . . Notice the solid ground beneath you and be aware of the others around you . . . Gently move your hands and feet to feel the life force flowing through your body.

(Pause)

Let that light from your heart continue to flow to the center . . . Feel your connection to the others in the circle . . . If at any time during this session you want to reconnect with someone, just follow that golden thread over to their heart . . . Let that be our main path of understanding today . . . When you feel ready, open your eyes and be present in the circle.

Take a few minutes in silence to connect visually with each person in your group and then check-in with one another, if you haven't done so already.

Guiding Principles to Establish and Sustain Resonance[3]

Review and discuss these principles with your group:

1. We shift our perception and identity of ourselves to one of being Essence, as "fractals" or unique pieces of one collective intelligence/body, "holders" of the frequency field, and imaginal cells unifying into one body.

2. We maintain awareness of our breath, consciously breathing, particularly focusing on the exhale, as this activates our parasympathetic nervous system, the grounding calming reflex. We experience our collective breath and move into the awareness that we are "being breathed" together.

3. We trust the all-pervading intelligence of the field and that we will receive exactly what we need to receive and know what we need to know in the moment. There is no preparation needed. We allow and open to whatever emerges or wants to happen next. We are open to outcome, yet not attached to outcome. We realize the perfection of this present moment.

4. Each of us contributes to the resonant coherency of the field—in sustaining, strengthening or lowering the coherency level. Our every thought, feeling, movement and word is continuously impacting the field. We practice increasing our awareness of when we drop out of coherency—such as through a quickened pace, a rushing, too many words, excessive movement, etc. We recognize this as it registers in our body as stress, tension, tightness, or shortening of breath. *We pause.* In this moment of pause, we breathe deeply into our hearts. We remember the appreciation we feel for one another and allow that appreciation to infuse our hearts with *love*. We consciously recalibrate our energy, bringing ourselves back to the present. In this, we hone and strengthen this meta-skill—the capacity to regain resonance.

5. We feel into, access and then speak from the silence and the intelligence of the resonant field. We trust the silence, the pauses, and the space between the words. We allow a pause to permeate the field between sharing. We let another's speaking/

3 Many thanks to contributing authors: Joanne Brem, Ami Marcus, Patricia Ellsberg, Shiloh Boss, Mark DuBois, and Brad Nye, in communion with Reba Vanderpool, Eric Lawyer, Claudia Welss, Gary Malkin, Davin Infinity and Sheri Herndon.

contribution "land" in the field. We respond to and from the field from what has come before, what is rising from within and what is coming through higher awareness.

6. We practice quintessential communication, speaking to the *essence* of what wants to be expressed from our experience in the moment. We discern between egoic motivation and Essence when sensing the impulse to speak. We practice perceiving the distinctions between noticing when we are attached or have the 'need' to speak and when we have something valuable to add. We recognize within ourselves and each other that there is equal power and contribution in embodying silence as well as speaking. In essence, our speaking serves to sustain the resonance, frequency, coherence and vitality of the field.

7. We trust the process and embrace any perceived dissonance in order to find a higher level of resonance through deep listening, understanding and returning to our still deep centers. Through our risk taking and being willing to lean in together, the stimulus and integration in the field provides material and fresh dynamics, which makes way for the group to find the next level of its evolutionary development.

8. We listen deeply—for the genius in what is being said and as if another who is speaking is bringing forth a needed piece in that moment. We listen for the transmission and attune to the frequency of what is being said, rather than simply the words being spoken.

9. We truly *see* one another as we cultivate the practice of witnessing one another's magnificence, genius and Essence.

10. We imagine that our collective intent is already done and manifest here, *now*. We experience what this awareness feels like in our bodies. We become familiar with this as our "new norm," and we act and speak from this awareness.

Building Trust in Your Group

For most of us, trust occurs naturally as we open our hearts and get to know each other. The more others open up to us and share their vulnerabilities, the more we open to them. *Creating a safe space of trust and non-judgment is the foundation of group resonance.*

Process: The Trust Walk

Read through the entire process before beginning. Allow 30 – 40 minutes for this exercise.

Pair up with another group member. For the trust walk, one person is blindfolded and the "sighted" person leads the "blind" person on a walk. The guide is responsible for the safety of the other person and should warn her if there are any hazards—such as steps, rocks, or steep inclines. This is most fun and effective if done in nature. After 10 - 15 minutes, reverse roles.

When you have both completed the walk, share your experience with your partner. If you do more than one trust exercise at this meeting, you may want to wait and share your experience later with the entire group.

Process: Trusting the Circle

In this exercise, the group forms a standing circle around one person in the center. Stand close to the person in the center, but far enough away that he can tilt toward the circle. Those who are standing in the circle prepare themselves to catch the person in the center by making sure they are standing firmly with legs slightly apart and with hands up and palms facing the center of the circle.

With eyes closed and arms folded across the chest, the person in the center allows himself to "fall" against the circle. The group members gently push the person back toward the center and another person in the circle. In this way, the person in the center is trusting that the circle will not let him fall.

After a minute or two, someone gives a signal to stop and the group gently secures the person back in the center of the circle.

Repeat the above process until everyone who so chooses has experienced it. Then share your experience.

Working with the Co-Creator's Agreements

Refer back to the Co-Creator's Agreements, which can be found toward the beginning of Section 2 of this *Handbook*. You will notice that many of them are related to honoring your Self and others and maintaining resonance.

As each person in your circle takes a turn reading one of them out loud, silently ask yourself the following:

- Which of these Agreements resonate with me? Which am I already practicing?
- Are there any Agreements that feel challenging? Which ones?
- Which of these Agreements are most important at this time in my life?
- Are there any Agreements that I would eliminate or change fundamentally?

When you have finished reading the Agreements, take time to answer each of these questions. You might want to write in your journals and then share with the group; or simply respond to the questions, one by one in turn. *If your group is aligned about making changes to any of Agreements, do that now; or agree to return to this process at a later time.*

Tips to Open Hearts in a Group

Although there is no one way to create group resonance, the following steps are suggested to begin the process of opening our hearts to others, co-creating love, and maintaining resonance in a group. Read the following aloud and co-create any changes that make them more relevant to your group.

- Feel the connection of each member of your group by holding hands, breathing together, and co-creating a shared experience using music, movement, laughter, singing, visualizing, a shared task or being in silence together.

- Create a safe space void of judgment for everyone to express his vulnerability, ups and downs, strengths and weaknesses. Give yourself and others permission to share your deepest desires, passions, visions, and insights.

- To build trust, allow everyone to communicate their truth often. Call for deep alignment and love and affirm the purposefulness and value of the group.

- Actively listen to what is being shared and offer compassion and understanding without judgment and resistance.

- Speak "leanly," avoiding long detailed stories. Differentiate between observation, discernment, and judgment—allowing for perception and comments without labels such as good/bad, right/wrong, should and should not.

- Don't project your own values, opinions, or criticisms onto others when really you are the one needing to make a change. Ask yourself, "Is this true?" "Do I know this to be true?"

- Avoid denial and openly share your thoughts and feelings to simply expose and release stored up energy, which may be causing separation. Take full responsibility for owning your truth in the moment.

- Know that you can actively choose to accept someone or something without necessarily agreeing with them or their ideas.

- Drop enabling behaviors. Each member of the group must stand on her own, to freely create and give unconditional love and acceptance.

- Acknowledge that you are the one who gives meaning to events. Be aware of the meaning you are ascribing.

- To re-establish a love space, it is often useful to have people move out of their heads and into their hearts and bodies, returning to their feelings and eventually their centers. This can be done by focusing on the heart and belly and by taking a few deep breaths together. It may also be helpful to have group members "check in" and speak their truth in the moment.

Guided Meditation: Shining the Light of Love

The facilitator slowly reads this aloud, remembering to pause between phrases. You may want to play soft beautiful music in the background. If you prefer, you can play the recording of this meditation that is available online at www.cocreatorshandbook.com.

Close your eyes, breathe deeply, and relax. Energetically, allow your attention to travel deep down into the heart of Gaia . . . the fire at the core of the Earth. With a deep inhalation, breathe the fire of life up through your feet into your body . . . Feel this heat, this flame of life, bringing vitality to every cell in your body. Continue breathing deeply as you acknowledge your interconnectedness with all of creation.

(Pause)

Now, as you inhale, expand your awareness and draw into yourself the vast universe beyond the Earth. Feel the solar system, the magnificent Milky Way, the billions of galaxies filled with more planets than there are grains of sand on Earth. Feel in total harmony with the universe . . . Visualize your Essence moving among the stars and the galaxies, as if you are visiting old friends.

(Pause)

Now allow your feeling for the whole creation to fill you with wonder and gratitude . . . Feel the Impulse of Creation expressing as you . . . Spirit manifesting in matter.

(Pause)

Feel your Essence expanding. Appreciate the beauty of all of creation. See yourself reflected in the light of love and affirm that you are love.

(Pause)

Filled with this love, let its continuous flow move through you and expand out to the Beloveds in this circle . . . to your family and friends, and out into the world. You can carry this feeling of being loved and of loving with you . . . Recreate this feeling at any time by taking a deep breath and experiencing yourself as an evolving aspect of the whole creation.

(Pause)

When you are ready, open your eyes, and look into the eyes of the others present—giving and receiving unconditional love.

Process: Moving from Head to Heart

The following exercise is a useful practice for coming back into center when you are feeling angry, depressed, afraid, or upset. By dropping all resistance to any situation or circumstance, you expand your energy, release stress from the body, and move fully into the present moment.

Select a partner and guide one another in this exercise.

Think of a time when you felt off center and were operating from your personality self rather than from Essence. Briefly share this situation with your partner.

Now place your hand on your heart and take a few deep breaths. Fully experience whatever feelings are occurring and be aware of any contractions you are feeling in your body. Become a neutral observer to the story that is unfolding. Don't try to fix or change anything that is happening. Simply be present to your experience.

Affirm out loud:

- *I am unlimited awareness.*
- *I am the open space in which all thoughts, feelings, and sensations emerge.*
- *I am love, peace, and harmony.*
- *I am all that is.*
- *I am life, and I am free.*

Notice that by releasing all resistance, the body sensations melt away and a feeling of well-being begins to emerge. Be with this experience of expanded awareness and neutral observation, knowing that full acceptance of any circumstance is a key to true freedom. When it feels right to do so, switch roles and repeat the exercise.

Building the Resonant Field Through Acknowledgement

Process: The Love Seat

THE PURPOSE OF the following exercise is to allow you to practice and experience unconditional love in your group. Before you begin, the facilitator explains the process to the group. *You might want to record this session, as you will each be receiving acknowledgment from all other members of your group.* If your group is large, break into smaller groups of 4 – 5 people.

A pillow, cushion, or chair should be placed in the center of the circle. If all are sitting on chairs, a chair of equal height should be used. Play heartful music in the background. Close your eyes and take a few minutes to open your hearts more fully to one another.

When it feels right, one person sits in the center of the circle, facing someone in the outer circle. Your eyes may be open or closed, as you wish.

Those in the outer circle take a minute to focus on the person in the center. Allow your inner voice to answer the question, "What do I love/admire/respect about this person?" When someone in the circle is ready, he shares what he is feeling about the person sitting in the center by saying, "What I love about you is . . . " "I acknowledge . . ." This authentic sharing may last one or two minutes. When the person in the center has received an acknowledgment from the first person, he says "thank you" and turns to the next person who begins to speak. The person in the center continues to turn to each member in the circle until everyone has shared.

Then another person sits in the center of the circle and the process begins again. If you are recording the acknowledgments, be sure to start a new recording for each person. (You may want to play this recording on a regular basis to remember how others see you.)

If it feels appropriate, share your experiences. What was this experience like for you? Was it easier to give or to receive? How might you apply this experience to other areas of your life?

Process: Acknowledging in Dyads

Form pairs. Sit across from one another. Look deeply into each other's eyes and attune energetically with one another. You may want to hold hands. After a minute or two, the facilitator asks that one of the pair speak to the other from Essence, saying and completing the phrase: *I see in you . . .*

Repeat the phrase with the different endings that occur to you spontaneously, allowing the love energy to flow. Speak authentically from your heart to the Essence of your partner.

After a few minutes, the facilitator asks the partners to switch roles and repeat the process. When both of you are complete, take some time to share with one another. You may want to write about this experience in your journal.

Closing: The Silent Greeting

This process can be used to close this meeting or at the completion of any gathering of family or friends. *It requires some preparation, as you will want to play a medley of beautiful music that touches the heart and builds group resonance.*

The facilitator instructs the group members to find a partner and to hold hands and look into each other's eyes. She instructs the group: *Beginning with this partner, you will greet each person in this group in silence, as though you were meeting them for the first time AND as though you have known them forever.*

Participants are to remain silent but will send love to one another through their eyes, hands, and hearts. Allow about 30 – 60 seconds for each pair to greet one another before moving on to other people. Continue until each person has silently greeted every other person in the group.

Note: This greeting works particularly well with groups of people of different nationalities who are unable to communicate with words but know the language of the heart. *Remaining silent and speaking with your eyes and hearts is key.*

Someday, after we have mastered the winds, the waves,
the tides, and gravity, we shall harness the energies of love.
Then for the second time in the history of the world, man will have discovered fire.

PIERRE TEILHARD DE CHARDIN

Deepening Practices

———— ❧ ————

The following exercises are to be done on your own.

ONCE YOU'VE EXPERIENCED resonance, you won't want to live without it in any area of your life. Patiently and with sensitivity, incorporate these principles and practices in all your relationships. You will positively affect everyone around you.

Living Your Values

Do your best to live from your values, deepest intention, and highest wisdom—without any attachment to outcome. Apply the Co-Creator's Agreements in all your relationships, including your family, friends, and co-workers. You might select one Agreement to concentrate on each week. Share your experiences with a friend, relative or other members of your circle.

Expressing Love for Yourself and Others

Every day, do something loving for yourself. You might make a list of all the activities that nurture you and make a habit of indulging in at least one of these daily: take time to be alone or with others in nature; read a good book; meditate; have lunch with friends; prepare your favorite meal. Whatever lifts your Spirit will serve your well being and that of others.

Appropriately express your love daily. A loving touch penetrates further than "skin deep." You can connect just as deeply through a warm handshake or a gentle touch on the shoulder as you can with a bear hug. The key is to feel connected to others in the moment.

A sincere compliment or loving words can make someone's day. When you are thinking loving thoughts about someone, share them with that person. Nobody ever got too many sincere "strokes." Tell people—your family, friends, or colleagues—that you love them.

An Attitude of Gratitude

Focus on the positive in each relationship and watch your love blossom. Set aside a moment at the same time every day, perhaps before you retire or during a silent or spoken "grace" before dinner, to recall what you are grateful for that day.

You know, when all is said and done, the only change that will make a difference is the transformation of the human heart.

JOSEPH JAWORSKI

Overcoming the Illusion of Separation

One does not become enlightened by imagining figures of light,
but by making the darkness conscious.

CARL JUNG

I tell you one thing: If you want peace of mind, do not find fault with others.
Rather learn to see your own faults. Learn to make the whole world your own.

SRI SARADA DEVI

The more we see the people around us from the inside,
the clearer and more compassionate our communication becomes.
This is the basis of a "new we."

THOMAS HUBL

*The fundamental problem facing humanity today is the illusion of separation—
separation from each other, from nature, and from our personal divinity.*

*It is this illusion that causes all criminal behavior, every war and skirmish,
the extreme disparity between "haves" and "have nots,"
and the disregard for and destruction of the Earth's environment.*

*Because the vast majority of all problems faced by humanity
are caused by humanity and by this illusion of separation,
the essential solution is the experience of union: an inner shift from
fear to love, and—most fundamentally—the consciousness that we are one.*

*This shift can occur "in the twinkling of an eye" or it may be the result of years
of deep intention, conscious attention, "due diligence" and practice.*

*When each of us accepts all aspects of ourselves, bringing the darkness into light,
we support the Authentic Self to take dominion in our lives.
What we do for ourselves, we can do for one another.*

*By forgiving ourselves and others and learning the communication skills that
are required for healthy, harmonious relationships, we open to seeing and
acknowledging the beauty that is the essence of every person.*

*We do our part to shift the collective field of consciousness from fear to love,
from a focus on "I" to include a concern for "we" and the good of the whole.*

Overcoming the Illusion of Separation

---❀---

We do not see things as they are.
We see things as we are.

THE TALMUD

FROM EARLY GREEK society through the time of Isaac Newton and the birth of classical physics three hundred years ago, most people have identified with their body and/or their thoughts and feelings and have experienced themselves as separate and different from other members of their own species. I-focused, self-centered consciousness has been the norm.

Newtonian physics leads us to believe that life is predictable and that everything is separate from everything else. Humans are like machines, cogs in a larger mechanism. Effects can be traced to a specific cause or series of causes, and it is only through effort that results can be achieved. From the perspective of classical physics, matter is the ultimate reality and humanity is at the effect of circumstances that are either black or white, good or bad.

This classical worldview prevails even today for most of humanity. Organizations and institutions are traditionally based on hierarchy and a strict ordering of roles and responsibilities, all based on self-interest. In this model, power manifests as domination over others, frequently through manipulation and control. Operating in these systems, individuals are often disempowered and their creativity is stifled. In gender relations, the male half of humanity is often perceived as being more valuable and important than the female half of society.

The sense of being a separate self stimulates competition and fosters a belief in scarcity and the practices of hoarding, exploiting nature, and valuing money and possessions above life itself. It lies at the heart of human suffering, environmental destruction, and most of the problems faced by humanity today. Whether it is the crisis in education, government, healthcare, or economics—the root cause is the belief that humans are separate from each other and from the natural world. This illusion of separation and its companion, self-centered consciousness, have proven to be disastrous!

It is not difficult to see that humanity is at a crossroads! We must evolve or face the prospect of perishing as a species. The crises we face are serving as evolutionary drivers, challenging us to wake up to our true identity. As Einstein suggested, we cannot solve our problems using the same kind of thinking that created them. We must shift from a consciousness of separation and fear to one of unity and love. We must move from self-centered to whole-centered consciousness. The Impulse of Evolution is nudging humanity to take a quantum leap in awareness.

Fortunately for our species and for our planetary home, a major awakening is occurring at this time. This current expansion of awareness was sparked, in part, a few decades ago by discoveries in the field of physics and the emergence of the worldview of conscious evolution.

A shift began when Einstein discovered that mass and energy are different states of the same underlying reality. Then science proved that matter can exist as either a wave or as a particle! What appears to be solid is composed largely of space—energy and information in motion. Reality is malleable and unpredictable! Consciousness, not matter, is the basic building block of all creation. Everything that is has emerged from no thing at all! Furthermore, everything is connected to everything else throughout the universe by an invisible field that holds the memory of all that has ever been.

Quantum field theory has collapsed the self/other, observer/observed distinction and has given us the principle of interconnectedness. The new science shows that every action affects everything else throughout the cosmos—that we live in a relational universe. There is no separation and no separate self.

When British biologist Rupert Sheldrake proposed his theory of morphic resonance, he suggested that a basic property of nature is that forms and patterns are contagious: once something happens somewhere, it can happen elsewhere—because the invisible quantum field connects everything. When individuals and small groups of people awaken in China or in Brazil or in any other country, that occurrence affects citizens of the planet in every nation. There are no boundaries when it comes to consciousness!

Quantum physics reveals unequivocally that humanity resides in a universe of infinite possibilities in which the observer creates reality. "What you see is what you expect." Intent—thought itself—determines outcome. Humans are not separate powerless "cogs in a machine," rather we are multi-dimensional beings, unique aspects of the Force of Creation itself. We can affect something from a distance by the use of thought alone. We are more than our limited beliefs, emotions, and physical bodies. We are incarnations of divine intelligence and are able to transcend the sense of being a separate self to experience ourselves as unique aspects of the One. As we feel our interdependence with all life, we naturally focus on the well-being of the whole.

As circumstances on Earth dictate that we must either evolve or face possible extinction, a new kind of human is emerging "just in time." This is the co-creator: a Whole Being who feels connected through the heart to all life and is awakening to the impulse to express unique creativity in service to the greater good.

No longer operating from a sense of separation, the co-creator relinquishes the need for power over others and celebrates joining in authentic partnership in a spirit of unity, love, and mutual respect. As a new norm, co-creators are able to bring love, coherence, and whole-centered consciousness into action, foreshadowing the emergence of the truly divine human predicted by Teilhard de Chardin, Sri Aurobindo, and other great seers and spiritual pioneers.

This is the world we are co-creating: a world in which everyone is living up to his or her full potential. In a resonant field of love, we support each other to be our Authentic Selves, discover our divine destiny, and overcome the illusion of separation. In an environment of love, safety, and equality each person's gifts can come forth to contribute to the creation of a just, caring society.

The exercises that follow in this chapter are designed to dispel the illusion of separation and to assist you in acknowledging your gifts and abilities, as you experience the joy of union. These practices can be used with your family and friends, your co-workers and business colleagues, within organizations or in established communities. With knowledge, sensitivity, and practice, each of us can support ourselves and others to be our best. From a place of love and partnership, the Co-creative Self can be liberated—allowing each of us to be free, to be fully empowered, to be great. We experience that separation is truly an illusion, merely a reality that we bought into and can now release.

By identifying with and loving the Self within and in others, we bring it forth. We learn from one another, acknowledging that each of us is a master in our own arena of expertise. We become mentors to one another, and we grow into our wholeness. Collectively, we move to a higher frequency of love and unlimited possibilities.

Guided Meditation: Exploring Our Values

The facilitator slowly reads this aloud, remembering to pause between phrases.

Relax . . . breathe deeply and invite any thoughts or cares to drift away, like clouds in the sky . . . Be aware of your heart beating in your chest and the life force moving throughout your body.

(Pause)

Allow the warmth of your heart to permeate your being . . . Feel a sense of peace and safety as you allow all distractions and concerns to be washed away with each breath.

(Pause)

Now take a moment to reflect on the values that you hold most dear . . . Do you treasure honesty? beauty? generosity? What are the values that you honor and aspire to uphold in your life?

(Pause for 1 - 2 minutes)

Take a couple of deep breaths and, once again, become aware of your body . . . and when you are ready, open your eyes and bring your attention back to this time and place.

Without speaking to others, make a list of your values. As part of your check-in, share these in your Core Group.

Communication Skills
for Harmonious Living

Abracadabra is an ancient Aramaic incantation
that means "I speak, therefore I create."
It means that language itself constructs reality.

RABBI ASHER CRISPE

THE IDEA OF learning to communicate effectively with one another is a relatively new skill in the arc of evolution. Our ancestors paid no attention to the "art of communication." Even today, most people around the world make no distinction between context, content, and process. They know nothing about skills like "reflective listening" or "conscious communication." In general, people talk and listen, project on and judge others, feel hurt and misunderstood, get angry, get over it or do battle, and believe that their sense of reality is, well, *Reality*.

It is only in the past few decades that large numbers of people have become aware of the benefit of learning communication skills to enhance productivity at their workplace and to engender a deeper sense of fulfillment and harmony in their personal lives. Today, many lawyers, therapists, educators, and diplomats make a career of learning and practicing the art of deep listening and conscious conversation. Non-violent communication practices, "transparent communication," and "compassionate communication" skills are becoming ubiquitous in the developed world. We are awakening to the awareness that clear communication, self-responsibility, and compassionate listening are critical skills for those who want to shift from ego to Essence, attain inner peace, and contribute to building a loving creative society.

In order to overcome the illusion of separation, we must learn these skills to communicate effectively with one another. As we traverse the sometimes circuitous path of shifting our identity to awareness itself, we begin to notice the aspects of our ego that feel separate or underdeveloped or even Self-sabotaging. We shine the light of awareness there. We observe our thoughts and "see our seeing." Eventually, we learn to embrace—rather than reject—those personality features that no longer serve our evolution. With practice, self awareness, self acceptance, and the support of our Core Group—we learn to love all aspects of ourselves.

The information and exercises in this chapter are designed to provide basic training in the communication skills that will allow you to discover and accept many facets of your personality and move quickly into an experience of deep connection and communion with others—Essence to Essence, soul to soul.

Tips for Healthy Communication

Discuss the following tips or principles in your group and, if you wish, modify the list in any way that feels appropriate.

- Truth is the rock upon which good relationships are built. Share your feelings and be honest in your communications, using "I" messages and taking responsibility for your experience.
- Listen with your heart; speak from your heart.
- Address only one issue at a time.
- Be sure that what you have to say is both honest *and* worth saying. If it does not add value to a conversation or to the relationship, don't say it.
- True communication includes body language and intent, as well as words. Positive intent facilitates the experience of connection or union.
- Timing, safety, and receptivity are keys to clear communication. Be sensitive to the needs of others before launching into conversation. Don't bring up important issues during rushed or stressful times of the day. Create a safe space for honesty and vulnerability.
- People long to be heard and seen, received and understood in their communications. Common courtesy, respect, and reflective listening are keynotes of conscious communication.
- The mind creates separation; the heart creates connection. If you are feeling judgmental, critical, victimized or separate in any way, try shifting your energy from your mind to your heart. Save your communication until you feel centered.

- Remember that genuine expressions of gratitude, appreciation, and empathy can engender the experience of connection and call forth the best in others.
- Do your best to reply rather than react. If you react, acknowledge that your conditioning has been triggered. Take responsibility for your feelings and your reactions.
- Silence is often the best bridge between hearts. Don't feel you always need to speak to be heard.
- As best you are able, be aware of your own growing edge. Do your best to avoid projecting negative thoughts and feelings on others.
- Stay current in your relationships. Unfinished arguments accumulate. Unspoken feelings can build in the body and create disease. The residue from unsettled questions can create separation in relationships. Be as complete and current as possible in your communications.
- Learn to make requests and honor your commitments to foster a sense of connection. Do what you say you will do in a timely manner to build trust in your relationships. If you break an agreement, acknowledge that you have done so and talk about it with the relevant other(s).
- Remember your humor.

Clearing

As we evolve and integrate our values into our lives, we may trigger unconscious internal reactions. Fear, blame, shame, judgment, feelings of inadequacy, and doubt may come to the surface, as the ego resists moving into new ways of being. The emotional body may go through a detoxification process to shed old patterns and assumptions. When we are allowed to fully experience feelings, an alchemical process can occur which frees us from the grip of the past.

When we do not accurately express our truth in the moment, this suppression of thoughts, emotions, or physical expression often accumulates and blocks the free-flow of energy, inhibits results, and eventually can even cause significant physical ailments. Telling the truth or "clearing" in the moment—and having it received—completes the expression and opens the door to a new level of relationship.

Tips for Clearing with Another

1. Time must be open-ended and sufficient and the person you are clearing with must agree to participate in this process. (If he does not agree to clear with you, you can practice releasing any feelings of separation using the first exercise provided in the Deepening Practices section at the end of this chapter.)

2. If there is very little emotional charge on an issue, a clearing may occur between two people. If there is a lot of charge or built-up energy, it is best to work with a neutral third party or small group as mediator. Agree that anything anyone says in the process cannot be used against them outside the session; that is, used for historical proof in some future disagreement. The intention of clearing is to disappear any suppression or limitation, not to hold onto it.

3. Before you begin, take a few moments for each person to center himself and to move to Essence (if possible). The person who has requested the clearing begins by sharing his truth (thoughts, emotions, physical sensations, and/or spiritual guidance) until he is complete, using the talking stick model. (See The Council Process in Section 2.)

   It is important to use the pronoun "I" in sharing, claiming full responsibility for your communication. Everyone else remains quiet and receives what is being expressed. As you speak, do your best to feel what the other is receiving. Be aware of the whole relational field and sense the essence of what's really wanting to be communicated. Feel into the experience from multiple dimensions, if you are able.

   If you are the listener, experience what the other person communicates as their truth in the moment. Take in their body language. Listen to the essence, not just the words or emotions. Know that a person's understanding of the truth varies depending upon their perceptions, experience, mood, and level of consciousness. Remain as detached and present as possible to allow for the clearing out of suppressed, accumulated expression.

4. When it appears that the first person has finished expressing himself, ask him, "Is there anything you have not been able to express yet and would like to add?" Allow him to clear out any remaining thoughts or feelings. As best you are able, listen from the other person's perspective.

5. Now it is time for the listener to share his truth, using "I" messages and taking responsibility for his thoughts, feelings, and reactions.

6. When the second person is complete, take note of the one, two, or three bottom-line issues that need to be addressed given the interaction. If it feels appropriate, acknowledge

your "soul connection" with each other and agree to continue now or set up time soon when it would be more appropriate for you, collectively, to seek out solutions that are mutually beneficial or agreeable.

7. In addressing the selected bottom-line issues, go within to that place of all-knowing, compassion, and oneness for a response to move everyone forward. Co-create solutions and agreements that express everyone's Essence and integrity. If your worldviews or deeply held convictions do not lend themselves to agreement, you can "agree to disagree" and still feel connected at the heart. (Remember, you are the one who is giving meaning to your experience.)

8. Acknowledge everyone's willingness and courage to tell the truth and co-create positive, forward moving resolutions.

Process: Practicing Clearing

Read through the instructions before you begin. Then pair up with someone in your group. For this practice session, it is recommended that you work with someone you respect and with whom you feel connected, *not a person with whom you actually need to clear.* This is a practice session and not the "real deal." Once you feel confident that you know how to use this process, you can use it to heal any sense of separation you may be feeling with another person. As mentioned in the Tips, if the situation is laden with emotion, you may wish to invite a third party to witness your interaction, be a neutral observer, and provide for a safe space.

Select an A and a B – or, if you prefer, select an A, a B, and an impartial observer.

A goes first. *Very briefly*, tell your partner about a relationship in your life that invites "clearing." (Ask yourself, "Who do I feel separate from?") Then take 10 minutes and practice clearing with your partner—as though he were that person. Follow the steps outlined in the Tips for Clearing with Another. Be sure to switch roles so that each of you has an opportunity to be A, B, and the impartial observer.

Whether you are working in pairs or in a triad, agree to fully share your feelings and then allow the other person to share fully without interruption.   When the process is complete, offer feedback to one another.

Were you able to use "I" statements? Were you able to come from a place of taking responsibility for your thoughts and actions? Were you able to avoid blaming the other person? Did you express as ego or as Essence? What was your partner's experience as you shared your truth?

When you are complete, you may want to write about your experience in your journal.

Even by practicing clearing with another "neutral party," you may feel a release of energy that has been blocking your flow of love. You may notice that you no longer feel separate and may not need to clear with your designated person; or, you may feel motivated to share with that person and move beyond any feelings of separation.

Note: If you are feeling separate from another person or a group, it may be best to take a step back and to ask yourself, "What is being activated in me?" "What in my conditioning is creating this sense of separation?" "How am I contributing to the bad feelings that have been engendered here?" By taking full responsibility for the part you are playing in creating a sense of separation, you may release the need to clear with another.

Discussion: Context, Content, and Process

Discuss the following in your group: Every conscious communication includes context, content, and process. Often, in simple interactions, the context is implied; the content is explicit; and the process is very straight-forward. For example, if a mother asks her child to "wash your hands before dinner," the implied context is her concern for the health of the child; the content is the words, and the process might include looking directly at the child, speaking in a loving voice, and communicating this message right before dinnertime. Process includes right timing, attitude, tone of voice, body language, and—most importantly—presence.

Being aware of these elements of every spoken communication is an important first step in modeling mutual respect and consideration. When individuals feel separate from one another, the cause of upset can often be traced to a lack of conscious process. For example, a family member might "borrow" something from another family member without asking permission, causing a storm of misunderstanding and accusation. In this example, taking a few minutes to ask permission might save hours and even days of hurt, blame, or finger-pointing.

The next time you feel separate from another person, reflect on the cause of this feeling: Was it the content of the words? Was the issue related to the process—or lack thereof? Was there a lack of appropriate context for the communication? What went wrong here? What can you learn from this experience?

Self-responsible
Healing Communication Agreements

THE FOLLOWING AGREEMENTS were created by and for Hummingbird Community in northern New Mexico, under the leadership of Ralph Huber, when a community steward. We invite you to discuss these in your Core Group and adapt them for use in your daily life.

- My intention for my communication with others—particularly when we hold different perspectives—is to achieve mutually greater clarity, understanding and intimacy.
- I take full self-responsibility for the feeling and perspectives I am experiencing. Specifically, I understand that I am giving the circumstances in my life all the meaning they have for me. I am responsible for how I hold my feelings and perspectives, not anyone else.
- I understand that someone sharing his or her perspectives is *not* telling me about myself; the person is telling me about him/herself—which diminishes defensiveness on my part and, in turn, helps to foster my ability to fully hear that person's point of view.
- I understand that the way someone else thinks and acts makes perfect sense to him or her, and I would very likely think and act the same way if I were that person.
- If I feel the impulse to change or fix someone else, I am watchful of my thoughts and words. I understand that I cannot know what is best for others. Therefore, I focus on telling them about me, not about them. (e.g. "The thoughts and feeling I'm giving myself about_____are_____.")
- I understand the value of *humility* when I am expressing my perspectives, realizing that I am not all knowing—not seeing the full picture. Remaining mindful of my limited understanding of the ultimate workings of life can help to keep me from "shoulding" on others and/or making a case/attempting to win a debate.
- I invite my Authentic Self's guidance and wisdom in order to non-judgmentally listen to another's perspective, as well as to truthfully and non-judgmentally voice my perspective—that is, what's alive in me. *I speak and listen from my heart.*

Process: A Two-Minute Release Exercise

The following process can be used with another or by yourself to shift feelings very quickly and bring yourself back to center. Select a Partner. Read through the following and then take turns guiding one another through the exercise:

Think of a time when you felt upset or off center. Identify the feelings and the body sensations that are occurring as you recall this incident.

"**What** are you feeling?"

(Pause and wait for response)

"**Could** you let this go?" (Are you able to release this feeling now?)

(Pause and wait for response)

"**Would** you let this go?" (Are you willing to move beyond this feeling?)

(Pause and wait for response)

"*Are you willing to let this go **now**?*"

(Pause and wait for response)

If you are willing, take a deep breath and step fully into witness consciousness . . . Notice that you have feelings and you have a body . . . but you are not your feelings or your body . . . You are the space in which thoughts, feelings, and sensations are occurring . . . You are unlimited and free . . . You are consciousness having a human experience.

(Pause)

Reverse roles and when you are complete, share your experiences with the group. You can use this whenever you feel off center—simply by asking yourself these questions and shifting your awareness from your personality self to your Authentic Self.

Forgiveness

Forgiveness allows us to make peace with our past and to be present and current in our lives. The need to forgive another arises when our unfulfilled desires give rise to frustration, confusion, resentment and/or anger. In essence, all of these feelings are states of mind, patterns from the past. Once this is recognized, there is an opening for forgiveness—a remembering that you are not the emotion or the story—but the space in which all this is occurring, the Self. This shift in identity is key to the forgiveness process.

Note: Forgiveness cannot be forced. You're simply opening your heart with kindness to those qualities in another that you reject in yourself. You are forgiving the actor, not the action—and you are aware that you have attracted this person and situation into your life for your personal evolution. You may even recognize that this person is reflecting an aspect of your shadow that you have yet to accept.

Process: Invoking Forgiveness

The facilitator guides the members of the group by reading the following, remembering to pause between phrases:

Think of a time when you felt "wronged" or misunderstood or when you deeply desired something and that desire was blocked. Briefly review the scene and the circumstances in your mind.

(Pause)

Now gently close your eyes and observe the process that occurred. Remember the feelings that arose— perhaps frustration, resentment, anger, confusion . . . Use your mind to track the process —to observe the play of emotions that occurred.

(Pause)

Stand back as the witness and allow the drama to unfold . . . Watch your ever-changing states of mind . . . Notice that when there is observation with no identification and no holding, there may be anger but no one angry . . . resentment, but no one resentful . . . Forgiveness becomes natural and appropriate.

(Pause)

Be aware of your body . . . How does your body feel? . . . How does your heart feel? . . . Watch your emotions . . . What are you feeling emotionally? . . Is there a feeling of contraction in your heart? . . . Is there a feeling of lightness or a sensation of release?

(Pause)

Take a few deep breaths and shake out your arms and legs . . . Become aware of the others seated in the circle . . . When you are ready, open your eyes.

When you have completed the process, turn to a partner and share your experience. Do you feel a sense of release or resolution? Has the energy connected to this situation been lifted? You may want to write about this in your journal and set an intention to fully release any emotion, thoughts, or body sensations that you became aware of in moving through this process.

Tips for Creating Conscious Communication in Groups

Discuss these tips and use them as a foundation from which to co-create guidelines for future discussions in your Core Group. You may want to share these tips with some of your other groups, if that feels appropriate and helpful.

- Select a facilitator to monitor the process.
- As a group, set a collective intent or purpose of your meeting.
- Raise your hand to be recognized by the facilitator to speak.
- Be present. Engage in deep listening at the feeling level when others speak.
- Be mindful of the amount of airtime you are taking to make a point; express thoughts succinctly.
- Use a talking piece, if this feels appropriate.
- Be open to hearing others' perspectives and, if necessary, ask for clarity to deepen understanding.

- Offer your perspective with respect and understanding, as well as openly acknowledging another's perspective. Tell your truth with love.
- See different perspectives as opportunities to strengthen relationships in the group.
- Let others finish expressing their thoughts fully before responding.
- Speak with humility, appreciation, and consideration of others.
- Stay focused on the topic under discussion.
- Set a stop time for each agenda item and if more time is needed, set a new stop time.
- As best you are able, shift from an "I" perspective to focus on the perspective of others.
- Hold an intent to dialogue for better understanding and deeper connection, rather than to convince or persuade others to accept your point of view.
- Remain unattached to outcome, as best you are able.

The Power of Acknowledgment

In Circle 2, Creating and Maintaining Resonance, you were offered two acknowledgment exercises. Take a moment to remember back to those experiences. What did it feel like to be received as your Authentic Self? What do you imagine it would be like if everyone in the world was fully seen, respected, and honored? What if we were all encouraged and supported from early childhood to do and be our best? What would society be like if each of us were living up to our full potential? This is the world that we are co-creating as we move beyond our differences and acknowledge the beauty that is the essence of every person.

We live in a culture that often ignores the beauty of our soul and focuses instead on our short-comings. As teachers, parents, and employers, we are sometimes short on praise and long on criticism, engendering a sense of shame and exposing a lack of self-love. The following exercises are designed to support you in shifting your identity from personality to presence and experiencing love and wholeness as the true nature of your being.

In order for an acknowledgement to "hit the mark" and truly touch the heart, it must be authentic. Flattery, which is transparent and builds the ego, does not support a shift in identity to Essence. True acknowledgments are powerful, nurturing, and often transformational. *You will probably want to experience one acknowledgment process at this meeting and save others to savor at future sessions.* Allow plenty of time to enjoy each of them and feel free to repeat them as appropriate.

Acknowledgment is a powerful tool in dispelling the illusion of separation, creating emotional connection, and calling forth the best and the brightest in each of us.

Process: See and Be Seen

Select a partner. Sit facing one another; hold hands if you wish. Close your eyes, relax, breathe, and center your energy in your heart. Feel the presence of your partner as the One expressing as this unique being.

When you're ready, open your eyes and look at your partner. Allow yourself to be open—to see and to be seen. See the timeless quality, the Essence of this person. Open your heart fully and allow yourself to give and receive love. Maintain soft eye contact for a few minutes, staying present to your experience, as energy flows between the two of you. Experience your oneness: consciousness meeting consciousness, love meeting love, Self meeting Self.

When you feel complete, take a few minutes to acknowledge your partner and to share your experience. Then, as a group, take a few minutes to look at one another around the circle— Essence connecting to Essence.

Process: The Angel Process

Begin by creating triads. The person receiving the acknowledgment sits on a chair facing forward. The two people who are doing the acknowledging sit on each side, facing the person who will be acknowledged. You may want to close your eyes to block out visual distractions. You can play soft, heartfelt music in the background, if you wish. Center yourselves and feel your hearts opening to one another.

Now, the two people lean forward and begin to whisper their acknowledgments into the ears of the third person. Both speak from their hearts at the same time, reflecting to the receiver all the qualities that they admire in this person. (Remember to be authentic and to avoid flattery.) Continue until you have said everything that reflects your genuine admiration and experience of the person being acknowledged.

Switch roles until each person in the triad has been acknowledged and finish the exercise with a group hug.

Process: I See You

This exercise is similar to The Love Seat acknowledgment process in Circle 2; however, this time—rather than a member of your group sitting in the center of the circle—that person will sit with her back to the group. Then, one by one—as you are inspired to do so, each of you will share what you most appreciate about this person, as though you were "talking behind their back." Repeat this until each person has been fully acknowledged. This can be a playful way to touch the heart of everyone in your group.

Deepening Practices

Following are several exercises to be done on your own.

Overcoming Separation

IF YOU FEEL the need to "clear" with another and that person is not available, the following exercise may be helpful.

Create a safe space for yourself where you know you will not be interrupted. Begin this process by fully expressing your thoughts and feelings in your journal. For example, *"I feel sad, frustrated, and separate from _____. I'm afraid that there is nothing I can do to gain his trust again."*

Be aware of any bodily sensations that come up for you. As best you are able—amplify, accentuate, and express any feelings and sensations that are there. Continue focusing on these until you sense that you are at the peak of your experience. Now, shift your identity from these thoughts, feelings, and sensations and focus on your Authentic Self. Tune into the qualities of this eternal aspect of your being. Affirm that you are awareness incarnate. For example, *"I am peace, love, truth, beauty, and wisdom." "I am All that is."*

With the power of intent, let go of your thoughts and feelings of separation and rest as presence. Feel your body relax and your heart open as you shift your identity from ego to Essence. When it feels right to do so, write about your experience in your journal. Then continue to identify with the eternal aspect of your being as you go about your daily life.

Becoming Centered

If you are feeling off-center, stressed out, or antagonistic, this process can support you to make an internal shift: to realize who you truly are.

- Begin by recognizing a stressful feeling. Notice how this feels in your body. Do your best to identify precisely where any tension is being held. Notice if there is a color or shape associated with this sensation.

- Make a sincere effort to shift your focus away from your analytical mind, disturbed emotions, or physical contraction to focus on your heart. For at least ten seconds, imagine that you are breathing through your heart.
- Next, recall a fun, positive feeling or an uplifting time from the past and attempt to re-experience it.
- Now, ask yourself: "What would be a more beneficial response to this situation. . . one that will minimize the feeling of stress?"
- Take another deep breath into your heart and tune into the wisdom it offers you. If you receive specific guidance, act on it.

Shining Awareness on Our Separate Self

In this *Handbook* we make clear distinctions between the ego/personality self and the Essential Self. This week, take time to reflect on those aspects of your personality that you have not fully accepted and may project on others. Examples of both restrictive emotions and limited states of mind include the following:

Fear	Self-importance
Greed	Conceit
Sadness	Blaming
Anger	Confusion
Unworthiness	Self-pity
Judgment	Dishonesty
Victimization	Controlling
Worry	Needy
Shame	Insensitivity

Reflect upon and write about the qualities that you are choosing to evolve in yourself and, therefore, embrace in others. As you shine the light of awareness on these aspects of your ego and focus your intent on releasing what you have been hiding, reflect also on the qualities of the Self. Place your identity and attention on Essence—that which was never born and never dies.

Forgiving Yourself and Others

In this exercise you will write down the name of every person in your life who you feel you may have hurt or offended in any way. Write down what you perceive occurred with each person.

Now, close your eyes, and evoke the presence of the first person on your list. Explain to him what you did, ask for forgiveness, and envision him forgiving you. Be sure to genuinely *feel* any emotion that is there. For a genuine release to occur, this must be an experiential, and not a conceptual, exercise. Repeat this with each person on your list.

When you're finished, write on the bottom of the paper: *"I forgive myself for all past transgressions and absolve myself of all feelings of guilt and shame."* Use the power of clear intent and heightened emotional expression to make this real for you. Then burn the piece of paper or tear it into small pieces and throw it away.

In the second part of this exercise, you'll write down the names and incidents of all people who you perceive have ever mistreated, angered, or betrayed you in any way.

Again, close your eyes, relax, and bring each person into your awareness, one by one. Have a dialogue with that person and express your desire to forgive and move on in your life. Bless them and affirm their happiness and well being.

Then write in your journal, *"I forgive you and I release you to be exactly as you are."* Be clear about your intent to let go of this perceived "wrong" and feel an elevated emotional response. As you do this, know that you are genuinely releasing the energy associated with each of these people and incidents. Then burn the paper in a small ceremony and take time to reflect on what has occurred. Your body and heart will probably feel lighter, as you forgive the past and move into the present.

Ho'oponopono

For centuries Hawaiians have followed a practice of reconciliation and forgiveness called ho'oponopono. In this practice it is felt that sickness or social disorder can only be healed and brought back into harmony by mental cleansing, confession, and apology. Traditionally, ho'oponopono involves family conferences in which relationships are mended through prayer, discussion, confession, repentance, and mutual forgiveness. The priest or kahuna, family elder, or the individual who is physically ill or emotionally troubled is encouraged to express and genuinely feel the sentiment behind these words, which are directed at the perceived source of separation:

- I Love You
- I'm Sorry
- Please Forgive Me
- Thank You

Buddhist Practice of Right Speech

Buddhists practice what they refer to as "right speech." By this they mean speech that leads to transformation and supports spiritual practice. The guidelines are simple and profound. You might want to put these simple principles into practice in your daily life. Before speaking, ask yourself:

- Is what I am about to say true?
- Is it kind?
- Is it necessary?

A Different Kind of Clearing

As you shift, change, and evolve on the mental, emotional, and spiritual levels—take time to go through your drawers, closets, and garage, clearing out any accumulated items that are no longer needed in your life.

Reflect on your relationships. Are any of them wanting to be released at this time? If so, let go of them in a loving, conscious way. This will keep your energy flowing, provide positive reinforcement for your new state of awareness, and open the door for more conscious people and opportunities to come your way.

CIRCLE 4

Accessing Inner Wisdom

Intuition is God in man, revealing to him the realities of being,
and just as instinct guides the animal,
so would intuition guide man if he would allow it to do so.
This experience comes in the stillness of the Soul,
when the outer voice is quiet, when the tempest of human strife is abated;
it is a quickening of the inner man to an eternal reality.

ERNEST HOLMES

Imagination is more important than knowledge.

ALBERT EINSTEIN

In the silence is the field of all possibility.

DEEPAK CHOPRA

At the very heart of the Co-creative Self resides an intuitive, loving, and comprehensive intelligence. We hear it as our inner voice, our intuitive knowing. It comes forth when we relax our body and ask for direction from within.

It hovers just beneath the surface of our waking consciousness, awaiting an environment of resonance and love to express itself in the world. It is amplified in a circle of trust and safety.

We practice speaking as this inner voice, giving it substance through the spoken word. The guidance for our actions is given. The design is revealed. The deeper plan for our lives unfolds. The word becomes flesh.

Every cell in our physical body has within its genetic code the plan for the whole body as well as its specific function within the body. So we humans may have within our "genius code" the plan for the evolution of the whole planetary body, as well as our specific function or purpose within it.

When we join together in resonance with other humans, we are forming a multi-human cell, whose nucleus brings forth and expands the unique function of each of us. Through the increased resonance and requisite variety of a multi-celled organism, rather than a single cell, we gain greater access to universal intelligence.

This intelligence comes forth as our inner voices, offering inspired insights which can guide our actions. Brilliant ideas begin to flow effortlessly. Deep insights suddenly explain unrelated experiences. Hidden truths are revealed. A critical mass of people in resonance will know the program for planetary evolution and the plan for birthing a new world!

Accessing Inner Wisdom

IN EVERY MOMENT, a source of unlimited wisdom and inspiration is available to each of us. This source has been called intuitive knowing, our inner wisdom, and "the still small voice of God."

It is not bound by time or space. We access it by quieting the chatter of our mind and going within to the "place of stillness." Although this source is always available, many of us do not listen because we are distracted by the information from our senses, our thinking mind, or the voices of others. Our busy and often stressful lives block our intuitive thinking process. In order to creatively respond to the problems that besiege us, we must slow down, relax, and invite our inner wisdom to emerge. To tune into the voice of divine intelligence, we must tune out the noise of the world and listen to the whispers and inspired insights of our Essential Selves.

In the past, we had to retire to mountain tops or hidden sanctuaries to experience a mystical state of being. Now we are making "ordinary" what was once "extraordinary." We can no longer delegate awakening to a few saints or mystics. We cannot turn to government, business, or religious leaders to discover what is right for us. Reliance on outside authority has undermined our expression as unique creative beings. We have also learned that logic will not solve most of our dilemmas. We are being called to direct our attention to our inner authority and to act as though our lives depended upon it. This may, indeed, be true. The time is upon us to consciously evolve a future that is commensurate with our love, creativity, and divine nature.

Our Core Group provides an environment of safety, trust, and love where we can practice accessing our inner knowing. The resonant field lifts all of us to a higher frequency. Surrounded by supportive and caring friends, our innate wisdom is invited into full expression. As we open, relax, and listen deeply, the knowing of our heart is easily accessed. It is the natural expression of our true, whole, and integrated selves. Sharing inspired insights with one another stabilizes our confidence in the capacity to access this part of ourselves. Over time, there is no experience of separation between mind and heart, inner coach and analytical mind. Mental chatter ceases to dominate our awareness. Complex issues are resolved effortlessly. Speaking soul to soul, our communications are rich and fulfilling. We are collectively lifted to a higher frequency as our Essential Selves.

There is a growing sense of freedom and stabilization in the emerging paradigm as we trust and act upon our inner knowing. Accessing the imaginal realm of all possibilities, attuning to our innate wisdom and following the guidance of the heart, we experience the dynamics of telepathy, synergy, and synchronicity. We are able to "divine the design" of creation and move forward during this historic era of planetary transformation.

As we stand on the threshold of the unknown may we collectively make the choice to trust our hearts, honor our inner wisdom, and allow ourselves to be guided on our evolutionary journey to wholeness.

Guided Meditation: Meeting Your Teacher

The facilitator slowly reads this aloud, remembering to pause between phrases. You may want to play soft beautiful music in the background. If you prefer, you can play the recording of this meditation that is available online at www.cocreatorshandbook.com.

Make yourself as comfortable as possible. Feel your body relaxing as you become fully present in this moment.

(Pause)

Feel a sense of lightness and general relaxation . . . Take a moment to follow your breath and notice if you are feeling any emotion . . . If so, allow that emotion to be present. Open fully to this moment.

(Pause)

In your imagination, see yourself in a beautiful place in nature . . . Notice a clearly defined path before you . . . and find your way along the path, moving toward a meadow ahead.

(Pause)

As you enter the meadow, feel the warmth of the sunshine upon you . . . Feel a sense of anticipation, as you know intuitively that your personal teacher or guide is waiting for you here. Your teacher may take the form of someone you know or this might be a historical or even a mythological figure . . . Your guide might even be an animal or an energy being.

(Pause)

As you sense who your teacher is, invite this being to join you, and take a moment to greet one another.

(Pause)

When you are ready, pose a question to your guide, feeling this presence as wise, trustworthy, and unconditionally loving.

(Pause)

Take in whatever answer is being given to you.

(Pause)

If you wish, you can ask another question. Your guide is here to support you totally. And, when you ask, you will receive . . . If at any time you feel you are not receiving an answer, be attentive over the next few days and weeks. Answers often come from an unexpected source and sometimes when you least expect them. Watch for synchronicities.

(Pause)

Know that any time you choose to be with your teacher, you are able to do so, by returning in your mind's eye to this same beautiful spot and asking this being to be present.

(Pause)

When you feel complete, thank your guide . . . Say goodbye and once again, make your way through the meadow, back to the path, and back to your current surroundings.

(Pause)

And now, be aware of the Earth beneath you . . . Move your body a little bit . . . and, when you are ready, open your eyes.

Take time to write a few notes about your experience in your journal.

CHECK-IN

As you check-in with one another, share any insights that came to you during the meditation. Did any feelings arise from reading the introduction to this Circle? Can you imagine a world where everyone follows the guidance of her heart rather than acting from childhood conditioning or the consensus of the collective? What might that be like?

Distinguishing Your Inner Voice
from Your Analytical Mind

WITH PRACTICE, EACH of us can expand beyond our analytical mind and access higher mind—the Essence of our being. We can learn to distinguish between the thinking mind that may be fearful, critical, and judgmental—and higher mind that is creative, accepting, and fully present in the moment. In the coming weeks, observe yourself and notice when your mind is analyzing and when you are accessing your inner voice—the still, small voice within.

Discussion: Accessing Inner Guidance

Refer to the following chart to clarify the distinction between the voice of Essence, the "inner coach," and the analytical mind or intellect. Observe what arises in your thoughts and emotions. Notice if you can hold the intellect and the inner voice in the same degree of love and acceptance.

There is a tendency as we shift from self-centered to whole-centered consciousness to have judgment toward our analytical mind. This may also manifest as judgment toward others. Review this chart and discuss how you can support each other to embrace and draw forth both the intuitive and logical aspects of your mind so they are able to work in concert with one another.

INNER VOICE	ANALYTICAL MIND
Intuitive and sensing	Rational and mental
Present	Past or future oriented
Unites; sees interconnected wholes	Compartmentalizes; sees separate parts
Certainty and peace	Can be confused and conflicted
Ease and flow	May struggle and effort
Acceptance and surrender	Discerning; can be judgmental and resistant

Focus on creative possibilities	May focus on restrictions or limitations
A quiet, calm, gentle voice	A conversational voice
Inspired insights; revelations	Thoughts and stories

Discuss the ways that you access your inner voice. How do you keep the mental body in check and tune into your inner knowing? How does your logical mind mimic inner knowing to serve its own ends? What are the different ways in which you receive guidance? (For some it may be through your emotions; others may hear messages or access inner wisdom through intuition; while those who are kinesthetic may experience body sensations.)

Think of people you know who speak and act from their inner knowing. What are the characteristics of their speaking? How are you able to recognize their ability to express Essence? How do you recognize *your* ability to express Essence? This practice of communicating the wisdom of the Essential Self—either verbally or in writing—is called inspired insights.

Inspired Insights

A SIMPLE WAY to begin sharing the insights of your Essential Self is to work with a partner with whom you are comfortable. *To prepare for this activity, choose a quiet, comfortable, and private space where you can sit facing one another.* You will be dialoguing with one another, Essence to Essence, and sharing any inspirations that emerge during your time together.

Process: Practicing Inspired Insights with a Partner

Begin by having a brief conversation to determine what question(s) you would like to contemplate. Agree on one or two questions that are meaningful to both of you. Choose which one of you will be asking the first question.

Now, take a few moments to center yourselves and place your awareness on your hearts. Close your eyes and breathe deeply, feeling a sense of expansion with each breath. When each of you feels relaxed and centered, you may signal the other by saying, "I am ready." Next, one of you will ask the question. Because this is not an ordinary conversation, you may be guided to sit together in silence before either of you begins speaking. When it feels right, begin the dialogue and continue until you both feel complete. Either of you might follow up with another inquiry, to continue accessing the promptings of your Essential Selves. Do not edit your responses or judge your words. Just allow them to flow naturally.

When you feel complete, open your eyes and share your experience. You may want to record your insights in your journal.

Process: Attuning To the Wisdom of Your Body

The purpose of this exercise is to practice accessing the wisdom of your body. The facilitator should read through the directions for this exercise before beginning. Your first step is to align on a question that is relevant for all the members of your group. (For example, you might ask: "What simple action on my part can bring greater harmony into my life?")

Begin by playing music that invokes slow conscious movement. *Stand up and give yourselves enough space to move around.* The facilitator guides the group members to place their awareness on their body:

Begin by closing your eyes and focusing your awareness on your feet, feeling your connection to the ground beneath you.

(Pause)

Now, slowly shift your awareness to your legs . . .

(Pause)

Now focus on your hips . . .

(Pause)

Your abdomen . . .

(Pause)

Your chest and arms . . .

(Pause)

Your shoulders and neck . . .

(Pause)

Now place your attention on your head and scalp.

Now the facilitator states the question and invites the group to move intuitively to the music and to access any knowing that the body offers.

Allow each movement to arise spontaneously . . . as the body wants to move, not as your mind plans the movement. What response are you receiving from your body?

Notice if you are feeling any tightness or discomfort. What is your body telling you as a response to this question? Is your body communicating any needs?

Can you express your current feeling state through the movement of your body? Take a few minutes to express your feelings through movement.

When it feels appropriate, the facilitator directs the group to lie down and to silently reflect on this experience before sharing in the circle.

Communicating Inspired Insights in a Group

Having experienced the inspired insights process with a partner, you are now ready to experience this with your group. This practice can be very effective when you are seeking clarity regarding right action for yourself or for your Core Group, and it is foundational for birthing a co-creative culture!

The steps for communicating inspired insights in a group include:

- Centering yourselves with a brief attunement to build the resonant field
- Formulating, clarifying, and asking a relevant question
- Moving into silence together
- Waiting for a response from within (inner listening)
- Sharing any insights out loud in the group

In this practice, you speak only if and when you feel inspired. It is important not to censor or judge your thoughts or the words of others. Relax and let the insights flow. One person's speaking tends to inspire another's and activates a co-creative intelligence. Some people hear actual words, some see visual images, and others may have an intuitive feeling or kinesthetic experience. When practiced over a period of time, this process can become the primary means of decision making for a group, as we will explore in Circle 8.

Process: Practicing Inspired Insights as a Group

Take a moment to center yourselves; then have a brief discussion to co-create the question(s) that feel relevant to your group. Once you have selected your question(s), the facilitator will offer a brief attunement.

For the purpose of this exercise, you might choose a question such as:

"What is our purpose together?"

"What is our next step as a group?"

If you want to focus on a transpersonal issue, you might ask a question such as:

"What can be done to support understanding and to foster empathy between Arabs and Jews in the Middle East?

With your question in mind, the facilitator offers the following attunement:

Close your eyes. Take some deep breaths and allow any thoughts to drift away.

(Pause)

Visualize or feel a glowing light in your heart and amplify this light by consciously breathing in and out through your heart.

(Pause)

Feel this light expanding from your heart to your whole body, radiating out to the center of our circle as loving presence. Sense the expansion of light that is emanating from the others who are present here . . . Visualize these lights dancing and merging with one another . . . Feel this glowing field of luminosity that is holding and connecting us as one body.

(Pause)

Now, the facilitator asks the question which the group has selected and then reads the following:

Let this question remain with you as you continue to expand . . . Release any thoughts about your response . . . Allow the answer to reveal itself.

When an insight comes, speak as your inner voice . . . Trust what arises . . . Offer it out loud to the circle.

Allow as much time for speaking as the group needs. You may need ten minutes or more initially. When there is a long period of silence after many have spoken and the process feels complete, the facilitator says:

When you are ready, return to this time and place and gently open your eyes.

You may wish to record any insights in your journal. Then share your feelings and experience with the group.

Note: The first few times you do this practice, you may find it easier to talk afterwards *about* what you heard, rather than speaking as you heard your inner voice. As you practice communicating your inspired insights aloud, it will become easier to participate directly in the inner voice dialogue.

Accessing the Imaginal Realm

Like many other highly creative and successful people, Einstein understood that the imaginal realm is where the most potent ideas that can change our lives or change the world are held. He knew from personal experience that nurturing the imagination by accessing this realm inspires creativity and genuine innovation.

As creative beings, we, too, can tap into this well of unlimited possibilities by diving into the imaginal realm—the intermediate region between the sensory world and the purely spiritual. We can apply the power of intention to bring forth that which is new and evolutionary in our lives. This is true co-creation: accessing the stream of creativity that is available when we look within, asking for answers or direction, and opening to experience a new state of being.

Guided Meditation: Accessing the Imaginal Realm

Before beginning the meditation, create a quiet undisturbed environment and invite each person to sit comfortably. The facilitator slowly reads this aloud, remembering to pause between phrases. If you prefer, go to www.cocreatorshandbook.com and play the recording of this meditation.

Close your eyes and begin focusing on your breath. As you breathe in, feel your body filling with life energy . . . Relax and let go . . . With each inhalation and exhalation, allow your body to open more fully.

(Pause)

Rest your feet upon the Earth with a delicate embrace . . . Allow the edges of your body to soften . . . Feel your breath moving in and out of your body . . . chest rising and falling . . . body relaxing fully.

(Pause)

Experience the miracle of life with each breath . . . and extend the gift of life to the trees and the plants . . . to all the kingdoms of nature . . . Feel radiant regenerative energy filling every cell of your body.

(Pause)

Attune to the deep knowing that lives within you, gathered through billion of years of evolution . . Experience the incomprehensible wisdom living in your genes . . . consciousness embodied in the matter of your physical form.

(Pause)

Recognize the exquisite coherence that is inherent in the great tapestry of life . . . Tune into the co-creative intelligence that dances through every atom and particle of light . . . Experience the force that unites molecule to molecule and cell to cell. . . Feel this force breathing through you. . . Know this as the presence of love.

(Pause)

Expand your awareness to the outer reaches of space . . . Feel your interconnectedness with all of creation . . . Experience yourself in this grand dance of creation.

(Pause)

From this place of expanded awareness, what is your dream for yourself, for humanity, and for the Earth?

(Pause)
What do you choose to create in the imaginal realm?

(Pause for 1 – 2 minutes)

What is your image of yourself as a Whole Being, fully empowered? . . . How does it feel to be expressing your full potential?

(Pause for 1 to 2 minutes)

Once again, place your attention on your heart . . . and breathe out a sense of gratitude and love . . . Breathe in a feeling of peace and well-being.

(Pause)

When you are ready, open your eyes and look around the circle. . . Gaze into the eyes of each other and recognize the Self . . . infinite presence in unique expression.

Take time to write in your journal any insights that came during the meditation, and, if you wish, share with your Core Group.

What I am looking for is not out there. It is in me.

HELEN KELLER

Deepening Practices

The following are to be done on your own.

Asking for Guidance

Silent reflection is perhaps the most basic way to access your inner knowing. Once you have centered yourself by focusing on your breath, be aware of any thoughts, emotions or body sensations that are present. Allow those to be there. Then ask a question that is alive for you at this time. A response may come as a sense of knowing, a feeling in your body, or in any number of ways. You may receive an answer days later. For example, a passage in a book might illuminate a perfect response or a friend might share something relevant with you. Watch for synchronicities and signs from nature. With practice and intent, your intuition will become more active in your life.

As your inner voice becomes strong—expressing images, ideas, words, or impulses—you might record these in your journal. Do not judge or edit these. Stay present and notice that true inspiration is fresh and new—distinctly different from mental thoughts that are repetitive and predictable! Revelation arises from the source of your being, guiding you forward. Like dreams, they often appear and disappear fleetingly if not captured in writing.

Audio Recording

Audio recording can be a very beneficial way to remember your inspired insights. Your entire mind "sits up and takes notice" when it hears your own voice speaking from higher mind. Listening to your inner voice seems to activate deep cellular memories. You gain access to deeper wisdom from the infinite presence that you are. The rational, critical intellect quiets down and listens, enchanted by the wisdom within. The intellect learns to honor this deep wisdom, using its powers to execute, rather than trying to lead.

CIRCLE 5

Ceremony, Ritual, and Celebration

*When your life is filled with the desire to see the holiness in everyday life,
something magical happens: ordinary life becomes extraordinary,
and the very process of life begins to nourish your soul!*

RABBI HAROLD KUSHNER

*Through rituals we open up to Divine Grace.
Consequently rituals are a powerful means of communicating with
and creating alliance with the Divine in all creation.*

TIZIANA DE ROVERE

*Initiation rites taken at the right time burn off what is no longer relevant,
opening our eyes to new possibilities of our own uniqueness.*

CARL JUNG

Ritual and ceremony empower our deepest passions.
They open us to a pattern that serves evolutionary processes
and connects us to the feminine aspect of our nature.
Rites of Passage help us meet the unknown and move
from one stage of life to the next with grace.

Music, silence, symbol, and myth
are used to honor sacred time and space
to anchor a new level of consciousness,
and to evoke archetypal energies.

When we bring our aspirations to life through symbolic expression,
we evoke the power of creation.
This is a realm for artistry, imagination, and genius.

Through ceremony and ritual, we can experience
ecstasy and union with the Divine.
We live our lives as an act of worship and
remember who we are!

Celebration is our offering of gratitude
for all that we joyfully receive!

Ceremony, Ritual, and Celebration

A DEEP HUNGER for meaningful ritual and ceremony pervades our society today. Many live in the experience of disconnection from the holiness of Earth and the deep feminine, that which embraces, supports, nurtures, and heals. The rituals from the traditions that we grew up with often do not feed our souls and enrich our lives. We feel the loss of not having relevant rites of passage to mark the important transitional points in our lives.

Accessing our intuition and imagination to co-create meaningful rituals, ceremonies, rites of passage, and celebrations is an essential element of co-creation. We draw upon the richness of our past and the wisdom of our ancestors to weave with the knowing of our hearts. Through conscious awareness and sacred practices, we experience the blessings of life and deepen our sense of interconnectedness with all creation.

The essence of the Core Group Process™ is alignment in relationships—with each other, with nature, and with the indwelling Spirit. From our daily activities—such as eating, gardening and parenting—to the uplifting moments of attunement to the Earth, we discover the good, the miraculous, and the holy in all our relations. We join together and rejoice as a collective voice in celebration of the preciousness of life.

Honoring the cycles of the moon and the turn of the seasons brings us into deeper alignment with the natural order. Ceremonies kindle a sense of remembrance of ancient times, connecting us to our roots. We are drawn into the experience of the feminine aspect of our being. An attitude of gratitude transforms each experience into a blessing.

Note: Unlike many of the other chapters in this *Handbook*, the ceremonies described here are meant to be used as the occasions arise and not as a series of exercises to be experienced one after the other. They can also be modified to suit other occasions.

Characteristics of Sacred Ceremonies

SACREDNESS

IN CEREMONIES AND rituals, we are acknowledging all life as sacred by honoring the great mystery and being present to the higher force moving through us. A ritual can gain potency through repetition if it continues to have meaning in our lives. For example, the ritual of expressing gratitude before eating or having a daily meditation practice brings intentional depth to our lives.

The repetition of a prayer at mealtime or ceremonies done seasonally can provide a stabilizing rhythm for adults and children alike. What's most important is that the ritual continues to be relevant, alive, and energetic. Although ceremonies may be spontaneous or elaborately planned, they are consistent in eliciting experiences that are both inspiring and emotionally uplifting.

SYMBOLOGY

Words, movement, and physical symbols are transpersonal and archetypal. When symbols are a used in consciously-created ceremonies, they add potency, mystery, and meaning to activities that might otherwise feel mundane or routine.

SACRED SPACE

It is important to give attention to the physical environment where a ceremony will occur. A beautiful and harmonious space that honors each of the senses will serve to set an environment apart from the ordinary. Candles, flowers, aromatherapy, incense, special lighting, music, bells, gongs, and items of beauty all enhance the experience of sacredness. Awareness of the temperature of the environment, as well as avoidance of possible distractions, are important elements contributing—or taking away from—the effectiveness of a ceremony. Turn off phones and ask family members to honor your privacy.

On occasion, it may be appropriate to create an altar which commemorates a specific situation, individual, or time of year. This can be built by the one who is hosting the gathering or it can be co-created by your group. You might ask each person to bring an item that is relevant to the theme to contribute to the altar. This could include a treasure found in nature, a statue, a picture, or a ceremonial object.

The physical location of a sacred space may be indoors or outside. Many people find that ceremony enacted outside in a grove of trees, a garden, or by a body of water, carries special meaning because it enhances their connection to nature. Earth altars, medicine wheels, labyrinths, and specially designed gardens can be created outside for use over an extended period of time.

Elements of a Ceremony

For a ceremony to be authentic and engaging, it is important to trust your intuition and personal guidance. The various processes may stir up emotional responses. Attune to the Essence of those who are participating and be sensitive to their needs. For many people, participation in ceremony and ritual brings them into unknown territory. Be allowing and gracious, creating a welcoming comfortable space for all who are involved.

In facilitating ceremony, you are dealing with alchemy and the possibility of transformation. It is like being a great cook. Look at the recipe, use your imagination, and then let it unfold. The amount of planning necessary depends somewhat on the complexity of the ceremony (for example, an elaborate wedding compared to a new moon ceremony). It is wise to think through details, estimate the length of time for each aspect of the ceremony, and consider individuals' needs for comfort—both physical and emotional. Pay attention to synchronicities and to what arises as messages from nature. As the poet Rumi expressed so beautifully, "Observe the wonders as they occur around you. Don't claim them. Feel the artistry moving through and be silent."

The following elements of a ceremony are offered as suggestions. Any or all of these processes may be appropriate at any given time. Remember to be flexible and attuned to the natural unfoldment of the moment. Most importantly, create a safe, sacred space and bring focus, openness, and presence to the ceremony.

PURIFICATION RITES
Purification rites are usually included at the beginning of a ceremony as people are arriving. They provide for a transition between the ordinary world and the sacred. Water, essential oils, incense, fire, light, and sound assist us in slowing down and becoming more present.

In the Native American tradition, the burning of sage and sweet grass is used to cleanse the space. Cleansing with water (simple washing of hands with scented water) or washing one another's hands or feet is a sensitive way of honoring participants. Blessings may also be shared by anointing each other with essential oil.

INVOCATION AND DEDICATION

What do you wish to invoke into your presence? What beings do you call upon for guidance and blessings? To whom do you dedicate this ceremony? How can the other dimensions assist you in that which you wish to bring into manifestation? In the ceremonies of many indigenous people, the guardians of the directions, the spirit of the elements, and the ancestors are invoked at the beginning of any sacred activity. A circle is cast and sacred space is consecrated.

ATTUNEMENT

The process of attuning brings you into alignment with one another, grounds you in the present moment, builds the love field, and allows for full engagement in the circle. Attunement can take the form of silence, chanting, conscious movement, guided meditation, or focused meditation.

The purpose of an attunement is for you to release tension, be fully present, become still, and align in resonance with the others in your circle and with the kingdoms of nature. The attunement may be brought to completion with a simple statement, a chant, or the quiet ringing of a bell.

CLARIFYING YOUR INTENT

What is the intent for the gathering? Focusing your attention with clarity of purpose will magnetize the intended result. When all participants align with the intention of a ceremony, there is a showering of support from the invisible realms. Stating a clear intent, in the present tense—as though what you envision is already so—is akin to shooting an arrow into the sky. Once released, the results are surrendered and the universe handles the details.

PRAYER OR BLESSING

There is an opportunity to extend blessings during every activity of daily life, be it driving the car, smelling a flower, standing in line at the bank, paying the grocery clerk, dealing with a business partner, or bathing a child. Holding the consciousness of extending a blessing, creates an opening to receive a blessing as well. Focused prayer creates a connection to the quantum field and affects the collective consciousness.

Song, Dance, Theater

The expressive arts have always been at the heart of any ritual. They provide an effective way to bond the group, release tension, unlock creative energies, and open individuals to their inner muse. Participation in these activities draws forth untapped potential. Exploration of the mythic realm can set a context to better understand your personal story. Song, dance, and theater always enliven any ceremony and create active engagement for those present. Music also plays an important role in creating the atmosphere and resonance for any ceremony. Take time to carefully select music to accompany various aspects of the ritual or celebration.

Closing

Just as you open any ceremony with an invocation and attunement, it is important to consciously close the circle. This can be an expression of gratitude for what has been shared and a brief prayer or benediction that releases the circle. You might want to hold hands and affirm your connection. The closing reflects the intimacy of your time together.

Guided Meditation: Feeling the Blessing of Being Alive

The following guided meditation incorporates invocation, attunement, and blessings into one process. As with any suggested process, please feel free to improvise. This exercise is best done holding hands, while either standing or sitting in a circle.

The facilitator slowly reads this aloud, remembering to pause between phrases. You may want to play soft beautiful music in the background. The facilitator informs the group that there will be an opportunity during the process for all those present to invoke into the circle any being or energetic that is benevolent and with whom they feel a specific connection. Spiritual teachers, archetypes, guides, or aspects of nature—when consciously acknowledged—are empowered into the process of co-creation. Examples include: Christ, Buddha, a master, saint or prophet, a mythological goddess, kingdoms of nature, and so on. Encourage individuals to speak freely into the circle.

Gently take each other's hands and close your eyes . . . Become aware of your breath gently moving in and out . . . With each exhalation allow the tension in your body to be released, as though it were flowing out from you and down a river into a vast expanse of sea.

(Pause)

As you breathe in, experience the life giving force—that which sustains you, the breath of life that comes as a gift to you in each moment.

(Pause)

Breathing in and breathing out . . . feeling revitalized . . . and letting go.

(Pause)

Feel your feet firmly planted on the Earth . . . As you breathe in, feel the energy rising up from the core . . . Draw the fire from the core of the Earth right up into your heart and allow it to radiate through your body, enlivening every cell.

(Pause)

With each breath, connect with the sacred web of creation . . . the exquisite diversity of species and kingdoms . . . mineral, plant, animal, birds, and those that swim in the sea . . . the myriad forms of life—all interconnected and interdependent. Experience yourself as integral to this mysterious dance of life.

(Pause)

And now extend your consciousness out into space . . . Open with each breath to the vastness of sky . . . beyond the beyond . . . to the starry realm and great central sun . . . expanding beyond our universe . . . with each breath relaxing, letting go, opening, expanding.

(Pause)

Resting in this experience of connection with all that is, honor your ancestors upon whose shoulders you stand, those who have carried the torch of light and shown the way through eons of time . . . Take a moment to appreciate the gifts of what has come before.

(Pause)

Invoke the presence of the spiritual beings with whom you feel most connected: teachers, avatars, great masters of our time . . . Softly speak their names into the circle.

(Pause and allow enough time for the invocation so that each person has an opportunity to speak.)

Now gently bring your attention back to the circle . . . Feel the hands on either side of you. Acknowledge the billions of years of evolution that have shaped these hands and created every cell of your body . . . Experience the fluidity of creation . . . as vibration . . . constantly changing, ever emerging.

(Pause)

Feel gratitude for all that has brought you to this moment in time, the continuity and perfection of your life experience, the grace that allows you to be present here . . . now.

(Pause)

Expand from this circle to family and friends around the world . . . Extend blessings and invite them into your heart . . . Feel your connection with beings everywhere . . . Experience the incredible web of light that invisibly surrounds the planet, uniting us as one family . . . Our circle is part of the intricate network of dedicated souls who are consciously bringing forth a new world that embodies the values we hold most sacred.

(Pause)

Feel the blessing of being alive at this auspicious time of our evolutionary journey . . . a time of transformation and rebirth.

When you are ready, slowly open your eyes. Look into the eyes of each person in the circle, silently affirming your love and connection.

Samples of Ceremonies

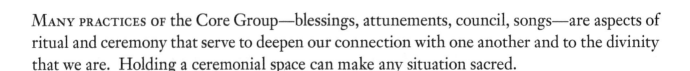

MANY PRACTICES OF the Core Group—blessings, attunements, council, songs—are aspects of ritual and ceremony that serve to deepen our connection with one another and to the divinity that we are. Holding a ceremonial space can make any situation sacred.

The effectiveness of the Core Group lies in its ability to be sensitive to the needs of the moment and to create a safe, nurturing environment. As situations spontaneously arise, the agenda for a meeting can be altered to address a specific individual or group need. It is important to honor the diverse traditions and religious and spiritual paths within your Core Group.

Healing Ceremony

Invite the person who needs healing to come into the center of the circle. He may either sit or lie down. Each person can gently put her hands on this individual. You may want to proceed in silence or have a facilitator lead a group process or guided meditation.

One simple practice is to act as a channel for Spirit by envisioning sending a violet light to the individual's body. It is important to see the person in radiant health as a Whole Being—rather than to focus on the challenging situation. The power of prayer has been well documented by scientists and scores of individuals who have personally benefited from this practice. If the individual is not present, the group can hold her collectively in their consciousness and send positive prayers for healing.

Ceremony of Empowerment

Use this ceremony when a member of your Core Group has stepped forward to focalize an event or an activity on behalf of the team. This might be a community event, a special project, or an on-going task. This person needs your collective support, encouragement, and vote of confidence. The Ceremony of Empowerment acknowledges that the entire Core Group trusts, respects, and aligns behind this person and the project. You could also use this ceremony when a member of your group has taken on a leadership role at work or as part of a community organization and requests the support of his Core to move into this new role.

Begin this ceremony by creating sacred space: move all personal belongings to another room, dim the lights, and light a few candles. Ask this leader to stand in the middle of your group. Everyone else takes his place standing in a circle. Take a few minutes to attune and build the resonant field of love. You may want to hold your hands up, facing the person in the middle of the circle, to send love and energy his way.

The first person who feels guided to speak acknowledges the leader, reminds him of his strengths, and affirms that he is there to fully support this person. As each person gives his blessing, the leader turns and faces them, taking in their words of encouragement. You may want to complete this ceremony with a celebration!

Ceremony of Differentiation

Make separations as sacred as unions. Whether a person is leaving a job, a Core Group, or a relationship—it is appropriate to recognize the value of what was experienced together. One phase has ended, but each person is moving forward to his or her next level of growth. Now there is a new relationship, rather than no relationship. The old way was to separate with animosity. The new way is to differentiate with love.

Create a sacred space that holds within it a positive symbol of your time together, as well as a symbol of the time to come. Create a ceremony that acknowledges the meaning that the relationship had when both parties had a common purpose. Appreciate all that has been learned, the gifts received, the lessons learned. Then acknowledge the differentiation, the natural changes that have created the new relationship. Express your present feelings of love or respect for one another. Ask for support in your next steps without the other. Commit to continuing to support each other as you take your next steps in life.

Ceremony of Commitment

After your Co-creative Core Group has met for several weeks, it is beneficial to anchor each person's commitment through ritual. This type of ceremony can also be utilized when starting any new endeavor—be it a project, an entrepreneurial venture, or a one-time event. Be witnesses for each other as you each light a candle from a central flame and state your commitment. When fire is used in ceremonies, the flame continues to radiate within you after the event. In future meetings you may wish to have a single candle burning, reminding the group of the bond that has been established, as well as the Spirit that connects you as one.

The Give-away Ceremony

The Give-away Ceremony is a rich experience of the joy of gifting and the magic that can occur as you gift that which has meaning for you.

Each member of your group brings an item that has personal significance and offers it to the circle. Gifts can be wrapped or not and offered to the circle in a variety of ways. You may each bring your gift to the center and speak to the meaning that it has for you, or gifts may be offered anonymously. Each person comes forward to receive a gift as they feel called to do so. Notice what feelings arise as you release an item that you may be attached to or when someone else chooses a gift that attracted you. (This process can be very revealing as to how you give and receive in life and how able you are to detach and let go.) Be creative and attune to doing this process in a way that best serves your group. Take time to journal any insights at the completion of the ceremony.

Note: The Give-away Ceremony is a poignant way to come to closure as a Core Group. Perhaps your group has done a retreat weekend together or you are completing the experiences of this *Handbook*. You also may choose to include the process as part of your holiday festivities.

Rites of Passage

RITES OF PASSAGE illuminate the next stage of our lives and orient us to the sacred nature of our transitions. They allow us to feel the companionship of a supportive community as we walk into the unknown. Those most commonly celebrated in our society include birth, baptism, Bar Mitzvah and Bat Mitzvah, confirmation, graduation, marriage, and death. Rituals help us to embrace change, let go of the past, and open to new possibilities. In a co-creative culture, rites of passage are recognized as being essential and occur at many junctures in life when an individual or a group is crossing a significant threshold.

Questions to Consider

- What is the significance and the purpose of this passage?
- What is to be recognized and released, and what is seeking to be born?
- How can the individual experience full empowerment to walk forward in strength and clarity?
- How does the community consciously witness and participate in this transition?
- What words, music, movements, and physical objects are symbolic of the passage and enhance the ritual?

Common Elements of a Rite of Passage

- Recapitulation and honoring of the past: walking the circle of our life in gratitude for all the lessons
- Acknowledgment circle: reflections from the community that honor the individual's qualities and good deeds
- Reflections from the elders: all those who have walked the path before us sharing the wisdom they have gleaned

- Statements of intention, dreams, and aspirations as an individual or a group moves into a next phase of life

Life Changes

Some major life transitions, such as career change, divorce, health crisis, or loss of a loved one, come unexpectedly and are often experienced in isolation. These difficult times are frequently accompanied with confusion, emotional distress, and fear of the unknown. It can be very transformative for an individual to experience the support of a loving community at such times. We feel companionship in our passage and can draw upon insights and reflections from our Core Group. Rites of passage empower us to access our own inner strength and wisdom and meet the future with intention and courage.

Stepping Across the Threshold

This ceremony can be created to honor a significant transition in the life of an individual, or it might be an honoring of a noteworthy shift for your entire Core Group. Beautiful ceremonial space is created with flowers and candles, and an item such as an attractive scarf is placed on the ground to mark a threshold. A circle is formed and individuals come forward, one at a time, when they are ready to state their intention and speak about the nature of their threshold crossing.

This may involve a sacred commitment or it might be an acknowledgment of a new stage of life or an important new awareness. Everyone present is witness to this declaration of intent and holds it in their hearts, much like one would do at a wedding when the couple are saying their vows. In stepping across the threshold, there is a sense of newness, like embarking on a great adventure in life. When everyone who wishes to has participated, close the circle in a way that feels appropriate, honoring what has occurred.

Honoring the Cycles of Nature

Deep attunement to the cycles of nature—the new and full moon, equinoxes and solstices, planetary alignments, lunar and solar eclipses—are foundational to any tribal culture. We have much to learn from our indigenous brothers and sisters who are living close to the Earth and are guided by the wisdom inherent in nature.

Discuss in your Core Group how you would like to relate to the various cusp points listed below, as well as other auspicious times in the year ahead. Do any of these times feel important to you? How would you like to honor the cycles of nature? As you look into the months ahead, do you feel inspired to gather at these times and create ceremony together? Perhaps you may wish to join some of the global movements and linkups that have the potential to shift the consciousness of the collective.

Below are a sampling of various cusp points and relevant themes for you to consider:

- NEW MOON: The focus of the new moon is on the feminine aspect of our nature. It is an opportune time to plant the seeds of new ideas, initiate a project, or open for inspiration and guidance.
- FULL MOON: The full moon represents the energy of fruition and completion. Each moon cycle has a unique energetic depending upon the astrological configurations. Take the time to celebrate accomplishments and affirm intentions with drumming, songs, and dance.
- EQUINOX AND SOLSTICES: The equinoxes and solstices usher in new seasons. They are signals to give thanks for the blessings that have come before and invite us to envision what we want to manifest as we enter a new cycle.

Celebrations

JOY, PLAY, AND delight (which means "of light") live within us as part of our essential nature. Cultures around the world have formalized celebration into birthdays, holidays, and special occasions or passages like promotions, weddings, and graduations. The core of celebration is giving and receiving love—expressing the language of the heart in any way that gives rise to joy, nurtures the soul, and energizes the physical body. In celebrating, we automatically release our minds, become present to the moment, let go and touch the Earth; we discover the extraordinary within the ordinary.

Just as you will want to integrate ceremonies and rituals into your Core Group practices, be sure to incorporate celebrations as well! If you have musicians in the group, your celebrations will be enhanced by their talents. You may want to set aside one or many evenings to share a potluck dinner and party together.

Cooperative Games

The following games are beneficial for bonding large groups who may be meeting for the first time.

NAME GAME
(No supplies needed.)

Begin by standing in a circle. The person who goes first says her name and demonstrates a gesture that expresses how she is feeling in the moment (for example: joyful, reserved, playful, quiet, contemplative). Everyone else in the circle repeats the individual's name and mimics the gesture. This continues around the circle until everyone has had a turn. You may want to repeat the process, as each person offers new gestures or movements. Have fun with this and use movements that everyone can duplicate!

STEP INTO THE CIRCLE
(No supplies needed.)

This activity is a great way to recognize what you have in common with one another. The group gathers in a circle and is instructed to take a step forward into the circle if the question asked applies to them. They pause for a moment in an inner circle and then step back into the larger circle.

Prior to gathering, the facilitator identifies at least 10 - 12 questions. These may range from simple questions like *"Step into the circle if you are here for the first time"* or *"Step into the circle if you have traveled more than 1000 miles to come to the gathering"*—to more personal inquiries, such as *"Step into the circle if you are experiencing a major transition in your life"* or *"Step into the circle if you feel you are living between worlds—with one foot in the old and one in the new."* Questions of a more personal nature help create a field of greater intimacy and safety. Participants feel more connected and relaxed as they recognize they are not alone in dealing with some of life's challenging situations.

BUILDING A WAVE OF ENERGY
(No supplies needed.)

Stand in a circle. One person begins by doing an easily repeatable gesture, and everyone in the circle repeats it 5-6 times. The leader then turns to the person on her left and passes the gesture. The person receiving the gesture transforms it into a new gesture which is then repeated by the circle 5-6 times. This passing of the wave of energy continues around the whole circle until everyone has had a turn offering an original gesture. The wave of energy builds as the circle becomes more connected.

KNOTS
(No supplies needed. A fun game for six to twenty people.)

Form a tight circle with your hands in the middle. Close your eyes, mix up your hands, and when the facilitator gives a signal, take two hands. If someone takes the hands of the person next to him or both hands of the same person, let go and reconnect with others. Now you're in a knot. Arrange yourselves in a circle without letting go. You may need to go over and under people to do this. You don't need to maintain a tight grip, but you must maintain hand contact.

RAISING THE ENERGY
(No supplies needed.)

Form a circle and hold hands. One person begins by squeezing the hand of the person on his right. Continue to pass the hand squeeze around the circle as quickly as you are able. Then see if you can maintain two energy pulses going in opposite directions. This means that one person will receive energy from both directions at once and will squeeze back with both hands. Now do this with your eyes closed. After about ten seconds, send two more energy pulses around the circle.

Deepening Practices

—————— ❦ ——————

The following exercises are to be done on your own.

Morning Ritual

Start each day in a sacred way with your own morning ritual that energizes you and connects you with the sacredness of life. Some examples are: communing with nature by taking a walk; lighting a candle on your altar and saying prayers; meditating and being still; reading an inspiring book or poetry; writing in your journal or recording insights; performing ancient movements like t'ai chi, chi gong, or yoga.

Look in the mirror and smile at yourself. Give thanks for the beautiful being who is looking back at you. Acknowledge that life is a gift and that each day is unique and will not come again. Listen to guidance from within as to how you might be of the greatest service. Set a clear intention that will carry you along with ease. Cultivate an awareness of the miracles that are present throughout your day and be in gratitude.

Evening Ritual

It's also important in the evening to unwind from the activities of the day. Breathe in the wonder of life and relax. Meditation, prayer, yoga, singing, slow dancing, sharing with a loved one, and journaling are all useful ways to come into balance before going to sleep. An effective integrative practice is to review your day by reflecting on your experiences from the end of the day to the beginning, like watching a movie from the end to the beginning. Reflect on lessons that have been learned and gifts received through the simplest of actions. Let this be a time to appreciate the contributions that you have made. It's very beneficial to be in a state of gratitude before drifting off to dreamland.

Cultivating Your Relationship with Nature

Any activities or practices which cultivate our relationship with nature are very beneficial. One way to do this is to create an Earth altar in your yard. It can become a special place that you visit often. Take time to be quiet and listen to the wisdom inherent in nature: the voice of the trees, the rocks, the tiny insects. Use your active imagination in having a conversation with the elements or singing to them. Recognize your place in the diverse and rich expression of all creation.

Another practice that is useful for enriching your relationship with the elements is creating a simple medicine wheel that is large enough to encircle you. Place stones in the four directions and embellish this space with other items found in nature. As you stand in the center of your medicine wheel, you can consciously connect with the elements and the directions and offer prayers in response to specific situations around the planet. You may want to feel your vertical connection extending out to the cosmos and to the core of Gaia. If you do this, be aware of your breath and consciously feel a sense of expansion and grounding. Tune into the horizontal field as you connect with all your relations. Extend your love to where it is most needed for personal and planetary healing.

During the day reflect on which element will serve to bring greater balance to your life. For example, it may be supportive to take a bath or to lie on the Earth. Perhaps your Spirit needs to be uplifted through dance or other forms of movement; or it may be most beneficial to sit quietly and attune to your breath. Notice the quality of interaction as you put your attention on each element: moisture on your lips, the sun warming your skin, the Earth grounding you, the breeze gently blowing across your face. Take time to appreciate the gifts that each element offers as you integrate diverse experiences into your life.

Blessing Your Food

Before each meal, take a moment to be grateful for that which provides you with nourishment and acknowledge the life processes that brought food to your table. When you are with others at mealtimes, join in appreciation for the food prepared with love, for the insights gained that day, and especially for that very moment in which you are communing together.

CIRCLE 6

Expressing Your Soul's Purpose

Finding the right work is like discovering your own soul in the world

THOMAS MOORE

*Each of us has a unique calling, a purpose that drives us to full
self-expression, a vocation of destiny. This urge to manifest our creativity
is as powerful as the drive for self-preservation and self-reproduction.
It is the motivation for self evolution.*

BARBARA MARX HUBBARD

*Not what you do, but how you do what you do determines whether you are
fulfilling your destiny. How you do....is determined by your state of consciousness.*

ECKHART TOLLE

Our soul's purpose is our innate calling,
the code of genius that brings us a sense of
wholeness and deep fulfillment when fully expressed.

It is the Absolute expressing as our unique Essence.
Our soul's purpose pulses in us with the fierce power that drives
the green shoots up through the frozen soil in the spring.
We are driven to grow by the force of creation.

We have known in the secret depths of our hearts the desire to be more,
to fully actualize ourselves—but for most of us, the time has not been right.
We have not been called forth fully.
The social forms to empower our full creative potential
have been missing. Thus, we've often kept ourselves in limited jobs,
doing repetitive tasks, and struggling to survive.

Now, we have entered a new cycle.
Evolutionary crises and opportunities are activating large numbers of us to
extend our lives beyond the immediate concerns of self-maintenance
and reproduction to the evolution of ourselves
and the development of a conscious, sustainable community.

We are at the threshold of the greatest release of
human creativity the world has ever known.

Expressing Your Soul's Purpose

*Every being has a definite vocation. It is the light which illuminates his life.
He who sincerely seeks his real purpose in life is himself sought by that purpose.*

HAZART INAYAT KHAN

ACCORDING TO THE Japanese, everyone has a hidden ikigai, "a reason for waking up in the morning." We refer to this as our soul's purpose—that which gives our life meaning and a sense of fulfillment and wholeness. Essence beckons us to follow our bliss and come home to our true nature.

Our distinct purpose expresses itself in sacred service—moving us toward full and passionate participation in life. Our true calling amplifies our Self-love and expresses our uniqueness, while serving the whole. It may reveal itself gradually over a period of time or may come as a powerful and sudden revelation. It may evolve and change. In any case, it is what gives value, deep meaning, and authenticity to our lives. It is always in alignment with our most deeply held values and brings satisfaction and integration to all aspects of our being.

In our culture, it is often a challenge to follow our soul's purpose. Many of us are encouraged to "earn a living" rather than serve the longing of the heart for true Self expression. To be faithful to our calling, we may need to overcome a wide range of admonitions and move beyond the narrow confines of our comfort level and personal conditioning. This will probably mean learning to tolerate some tension and ambiguity as we begin to clarify our deeper reason for being. As we allow the powerful call of the soul to move us, it may be necessary to drop the need for approval, to resist the expectation to conform to someone else's standards, and to overcome the fear of change and the unknown. Sometimes the discovery of our soul's purpose is preceded by a life crisis and a great humbling of the ego.

In following our purpose, we may be motivated to excel at something we are doing already; or we may seek new work or creative expression. Some of us may pioneer new social functions or create innovative enterprises.

We recognize that, at this stage of evolution, many of us are pursuing a job or vocation that pays the bills, while we "moonlight" at that which genuinely gives our life a sense of meaning. As pioneers entering a new paradigm, we may be waiting for right timing to fully give our gifts in the world and to be appropriately compensated for our service.

To fully express our purpose, we need to collaborate with others whose creativity sparks our own. This is why Core Groups are a perfect environment for the emergence and stabilization of our life purpose. Resonance, unconditional love, and inspired insights unlock our potential. Deep interactions stimulate creativity and support the ongoing processes of Self-discovery and Self-actualization.

Wherever we are fully expressing ourselves and empowering others in our true purposes, we are on the front lines of evolutionary change. We are embodying the knowing that each of us is an expression of the Infinite, here to play our role in this divine dance called life. We are opening the way for others to follow their hearts and fulfill their destiny.

Many decades ago psychologist Abraham Maslow stated that human motivation is based on people seeking fulfillment and change through personal growth. In mapping his "hierarchy of needs" model, he studied the positive potential of human beings and discovered that a key to happiness is to find chosen work that is Self-rewarding and of service to at least one other person. We call this "expressing your soul's purpose!"

Guided Meditation: Discovering Your Soul's Purpose

Before beginning the meditation, make sure to have your journal and pen handy to write down any insights you receive during this process. The facilitator reads this aloud, remembering to pause between phrases. You may want to play soft, beautiful music in the background. If you prefer, you can play the recording of this guided meditation that is available at www.cocreatorshandbook.com.

Close your eyes, relax, and invite your mind to be still . . . Feel at peace as you connect with the Earth and the cosmos through your breath . . . Breathe in and out through your heart . . . Feel your energy expanding and merging with all kingdoms of this planet and beyond . . . Breathe deeply as a being who is one with all.

(Pause)

Now, think of a time when you felt totally fulfilled . . . when life felt meaningful and you were giving your best . . . What were you doing?

(Pause for 1 minute)

Where do your interests lie?. . . What are your passions in life?

(Pause for 1 – 2 minutes)

Have you ever felt in total alignment with your true nature?. . . What was that like for you? . . . What were you doing?

(Pause for 1 – 2 minutes)

Now take a few moments to reflect on your gifts and talents . . . Where do you experience mastery in your life? . . . What do you do effortlessly and naturally? . . . What are your greatest strengths?

(Pause for 1 – 2 minutes)

What forms of creative expression bring you joy?

(Pause for 1 minute)

If money were no object, what would you be doing?

(Pause for 1 minute)

If you had one year to live, what would you do? . . . Who would you choose to be with?

(Pause for 1 minute)

Take a few deep breaths and become aware of your surroundings . . . If you are feeling any sensations in your body, notice where you are feeling them.

(Pause)

When you are ready, open your eyes and capture your insights in your journal. Stay in your center in silence.

As you reflect on the insights you received during this guided meditation, see if you can begin to formulate your soul's purpose.

Take about 10 – 15 minutes to write down your answers to the following:

- When I think about my life purpose, I feel . . .
- The primary strengths I have to accomplish my purpose in life are . . .
- The self-imposed, limiting beliefs that seem to be blocking me are . . .
- The external blocks that seem to be in my path are . . .
- I can begin to overcome these blocks by . . .
- Others in the group can support me in overcoming these blocks by . . .

Share with your group what you have discovered, and do not judge yourself or others for where you are in the process of discovering your soul's calling.

Identifying Your Soul's Purpose

Discuss the following with your group and make any changes or additions that are in keeping with your deeper knowing or experience.

How do you know you are on the "right track"— pursuing your true purpose in life?

You will know when:

- Your work feels like play and is aligned with your deepest values
- You can't "not do" what you are doing; it flows from your being
- You have a feeling of "fit" and authenticity
- Your outer world reflects your inner experience and knowing
- You feel energized and fulfilled, guided intuitively in expressing your creativity
- Your obstacles are minimal
- Your life flows with synchronicities
- Your part supports the well being of the whole

Calling on Your Clearness Committee

In his excellent book *Callings*, Gregg Levoy mentions Quaker "clearness committees," which assist members to gain clarity about important issues in their lives. In the following exercise, your Core Group will serve this function. You might reserve one full meeting for this exercise, if many members need support in discovering their true calling.

Process: Discovering Your Soul's Purpose

Read through these instructions before beginning. You may find it helpful to record this process. Any member of your circle who needs to gain clarity regarding his soul's calling can be the "focus person" in this exercise. You may sit in the middle of the circle, if you wish. Begin by explaining concisely what you need from the group.

Observe a few minutes of silence together, consciously building the resonant field, with all members asking for guidance for the person in the center of the circle. In response to what the "focus person" has indicated he wants from the group, other members ask questions *and refrain from making any editorial comments.*

The questions might include:

- What do you feel passionate about?
- What activities or circumstances bring you joy?
- How do you love to serve?
- Where and how do you excel?
- When you reflect on your childhood, what were your natural talents?

Do not censor or judge your questions. All questions that arise in response to this member's request are valid. Do not give advice, try to solve problems, or tell stories. Know that the answer will come from the person seeking clarity.

As the focus person, respond as you wish to the questions being posed. It may be helpful to reflect on some of the questions and write your answers in your journal at a later time. Be patient with your own evolution. Your heart must be ready and events may need to unfold before you are able to find your true place of service and creative expression. Allow each person who chooses to do so to take a turn being the focus person in the circle.

Note: Gregg Levoy suggests that clues related to your soul's calling may be found in recurring dreams, overheard conversations, a chance meeting that sparks something new in you, synchronicities, song lyrics you can't get out of your head, instructions that arise from silence, or issues that are waiting for resolution. Stay alert for signs that are mysteriously guiding you to your deeper life purpose.

Process: A Call from Your Future Self

The important point is that in exploring this future potential,
you aren't exploring a future someone else has written for you.
It's more intimately connected with your evolving, Authentic Self—
who you really are. It's much more fluid, more open,
more in dialogue with you. This is why Martin Buber
said it stands in need of you in order to be born.

OTTO SCHARMER

In this process you will be entertaining the possibility that something is streaming toward you from the future: a destiny call—an energy that calls you forward. The purpose of this exercise is to access guidance from your future Self, to listen deeply to your destiny call. Allow 15 minutes for this process and ask someone to be the timekeeper.

Find a partner and sit facing each other. Look deeply into each other's eyes and connect heart to heart. Practice the Heart Meditation with one another for a few minutes.

Partner A begins by asking Partner B: "What calls you?" Partner B responds. Partner A says, "Thank you" and then asks again, "What calls you?"

This sequence continues for 2-3 minutes, allowing Partner B to respond with whatever arises. Do not consciously "think" about it, just say whatever comes to you.

After a few minutes, the timekeeper signals you to stop and reverse roles. It's beneficial for each person to have several turns, allowing the experience to deepen. Take time at the completion to share your experience and/or write in your journal.

Guided Meditation: Taking a Mythic Journey

This exercise allows you to review your life as a hero's or heroine's journey. In this guided meditation, the treasure you seek is your true purpose. The obstacles you have faced are the initiations, tests, and heroic struggles you have endured.

Select a partner. You will take turns reading the following to one another and writing your partner's response in her journal. Make sure you are far enough away from other members of your group to maintain a sense of privacy. If you feel comfortable doing so, it helps to lie down for this exercise. You will need at least 40 minutes, allowing 20 minutes for each person. Decide who will go first and create a comfortable space. Partner A begins by reading the following, remembering to pause between phrases:

Gently close your eyes and feel the floor supporting your body . . . Follow your breath, as you relax deeply and quiet your thoughts . . . Allow for more spaciousness in your mind and your body . . . Release any tension you may be feeling.

(Pause)

Continue to breathe deeply and envision a cloud of pink light surrounding your body.

(Pause)

Let go and feel the warmth and safety of your surroundings, as you relax even more fully as Essence . . .

(Pause)

Now place your awareness on your body and see yourself lying in this room . . . You are about to take a journey in your imagination . . . a hero's (or heroine's) journey.

(Pause)

Imagine that you are preparing to incarnate on this planet . . . Imagine that, as a soul, you are choosing your parents and the life situation that will provide the greatest teachings in service to the evolution of your consciousness.

(Pause)

Allow any images of your descent into form to emerge . . . Was your birth a gentle one or was it challenging? Were you comfortable in your body or did you feel resistance or a sense of limitation?

(Pause)

Connect with your early childhood and original innocence . . . What images arise? Did you feel connected with nature and life around you? Are there distinct memories that have shaped your reality today?

(Pause)

What is your mythic name? . . . Who are your allies?. . . What obstacles, if any, did you face as a child?

(Pause for 1 – 2 minutes)

Now see this hero (or heroine) that you are as a young person, a teenager. . . Who are your teachers and guides? . . . What are you learning?. . . What brings you the greatest fulfillment and joy?

(Pause for 1 – 2 minutes)

And now envision this hero/heroine as an adult . . . What archetypes have you played out in this life? . . . the battle between good and evil? . . . death and resurrection? . . . betrayal and forgiveness?. . . What are the lessons of life that feel most predominant?

(Pause for 1 – 2 minutes)

What is the theme of your present search or challenge? . . . Are you letting go? . . . Are you waking up? . . . Are you discovering your heart's calling? . . . Are you giving your unique gifts?

(Pause for 1 – 2 minutes)

Who are your allies today? . . . What obstacles face you from within and without?. . . Is there a treasure that you are seeking to find?

(Pause for 1 – 2 minutes)

How have you changed in the past year? . . . What is being born in you? . . . What, if anything, wants to be released?

(Pause for 1 – 2 minutes)

Are you being asked to make significant shifts in the course of your life? . . . If so, are you willing to do so?

(Pause)

Take a few deep breaths and become aware of your body lying in this room . . . Feel the presence of the other people nearby.

(Pause)

When you're ready, gently open your eyes and take a few minutes to reflect on your insights and experience before reversing roles with your partner.

Sharing to Clarify Your Life's Purpose

At your next meeting or in the coming weeks, help each other gain greater clarity about your chosen work through coaching and inspired insights. You might ask: *"With whom do I need to connect now?"* or *"What is my next step?"* This process, if done in depth, could be the focus of an entire session.

Re-forming Your Core Group

Now THAT YOU have a sense of *what* you want to express, the next question is *who* are your natural partners? As attracted as you may be to the people in your initial Core Group, they may not all be your vocational partners. *They probably are not.*

If your life purpose is not fulfilled in a particular Core, it is wise for you to create a new one that is more empowering. Remember that we are in the process of building a new social body with a number of parts that is almost infinite. No one will be left out. Each of us has a unique gift that is needed to build this new body. It is better to separate now and form a new group, rather than to disempower yourself by ignoring your vocational needs and your internal guidance. Your lack of enthusiasm can affect the effectiveness of the group.

This process of re-formation is called "differentiation." Nature differentiates according to specific functions. Each atom, cell, human, and Core Group has its own unique properties and gifts to give to the planetary body. Dysfunction occurs when cells are not in their appropriate places. In the same way, differentiation will help you find the right teammates who share your life purpose so that you can be fully supported, actualized, and successful in your correct and freely-chosen functions.

Note: If each person in your circle has a sense of unique purpose, this is probably the time to move from your Resonant Core into new Co-creative Cores, in order for each of you to fully express your potential with others who share your soul's calling. Although you can complete this entire *Handbook* with your original Core Group, it is probably more satisfying and productive to differentiate and create another circle with individuals who share your deeper life purpose. Review and discuss the following Tips for Differentiation before forming new Co-creative Core Groups.

Tips for Differentiation

- As you explore connecting with others who share your vision and mission, create an "engagement" period to allow for experimentation before committing to a specific project. Be attentive to resonance and aligned purpose as you reach out to others to form a new Core. This is like dating: you may need to try out different relationships until you find the ones that feel like a perfect fit.
- Be patient, non-judgmental, and compassionate during this process. Trust that you and all other members of your Core will find your perfect place in the larger pattern.
- Make sure that you and everyone else involved in your new Core feels totally safe in telling your truth—if people, the situation, or actions are not working. Find solutions that work for everyone including re-formation of groups, if necessary.
- Respect the domain and function of each person and group. All gifts are needed to birth a new, more loving world.
- You must have an affinity for each member of your Core and a respect for your differences. If personal conflicts arise and persist after clearing, it may be appropriate to separate and re-form the group(s).
- Spending much of your time "processing" is an indication that you have not found your perfect partners. Right relationship fosters ease, grace, playfulness, and humor. Persistent lack of resonance is a strong indication that differentiation should be considered.
- Over-inclusion (so no one will feel "left out") can reduce the resonance and effectiveness of your group.
- Make sure each of you is aligned with and actualized by your shared purpose and that the size of your group supports its functions. Too large a group can be unwieldy and stifling of individual creative expression.

Re-evaluate and Re-choose

As you differentiate, you may want to re-evaluate the meeting format of your new group. Perhaps a structure that is different from the one you have now would function better as you move into a co-creative project or business. For example, if you've been meeting weekly, your Co-creative Core may find it more effective to meet for one full day every other week.

As you evolve, your purpose evolves. What you are drawn to today may be fully satisfying this month but not feel accurate next year. Yet what you do today may be essential to building the skills and the personal strength to do tomorrow's work. This choosing and re-choosing is an ongoing process that will evolve naturally and organically.

If you do create a new group, be sure to practice at least some of the exercises from each of the first four Circles of this book throughout your "courtship" period. Become "engaged" long enough to find out if your new group is the right Core for each of you to fulfill your destiny. Deep bonding creates an essential foundation for effective, sustainable work in the world.

Draw on the Ceremony of Differentiation in Circle 5, if you feel it is time to re-form into different groups. Acknowledge your deep soul connection to one another as you step from this group to work with another team. Differentiation does not imply separation. It is simply a movement into right relationship based on your shared destiny. If done consciously with full communication, it is natural and fulfilling for all group members.

Discuss with your circle how you want to proceed from here. You may want to do an inspired insights exercise, asking for guidance in making this decision.

Ceremony of Divine Destiny

It is recommended that this ceremony be enacted at the completion of Circle 6. Although this ceremony is very similar to the process in Circle 5 called Stepping Across the Threshold, the focus this time is on acknowledging each person's unique calling.

Create sacred space with soft, beautiful music playing in the background. Ask each member of your group to come forward, one at a time, and declare the insights they have received in regards to discovering their soul's purpose. For some individuals, the sense of purpose might be general—like "uplifting consciousness through regular prayer and by extending blessings." For others, your purpose may be very specific—such as "developing technologies to support handicapped children in the developing world."

The Ceremony of Divine Destiny may involve taking a specific next step or it might be a bold declaration of soul's purpose. Those present are sacred witnesses, holding loving presence for the individual as each person makes a statement about her soul's calling.

Awakened doing is the alignment of your outer purpose—what you do—
with your inner purpose—awakening and staying awake.
Through awakened doing, you become one with the outgoing purpose of the universe.
Consciousness flows through you into this world.

ECKHART TOLLE

Deepening Practices

The following exercises are to be done on your own.

Embracing Your Soul's Journey

IF YOU ARE still not clear about your soul's calling, write or record your life story. Look for recurring themes that might point toward your purpose: high points, fulfilling moments, experiences that felt expansive and exhilarating. Assess yourself and describe your personal qualities. What qualities do you want to enhance? Acknowledge the perfection of all aspects of your soul's journey, including the struggles, difficulties, and challenges.

Next, have an inner dialogue about your true purpose. Use the questions that follow to stir your soul. This exercise is similar to the mythic journey you did with a partner; however, in this exercise you are focusing on your spiritual/psychological/physical journey—rather than on your mythic journey.

Ask yourself the following questions and write down or record your answers:

- What are my gifts?
- Where and how do I excel?
- What gives me great satisfaction?
- What do I feel really passionate about?
- What are my most beloved pursuits?
- What "business" am I in? What is it that I'm about?
- Have I ever done anything that felt like I was making a contribution? What was it?
- When I have felt totally successful and joyful, what was I doing?
- What reflections have I received from others that reflect my uniqueness?
- When have I been able to sustain a high level of performance with a high level of personal energy? What are the characteristics of these times: the work, the people, the physical environment, the results?
- If I could wave a magic wand and all the conditions were right (family, education, time, money), what would I be doing with my life?
- What limiting beliefs or fears are blocking me from discovering and fulfilling my true purpose?

Relax and do not force the answers, but—over a period of time—ask for clarity and guidance regarding your soul's purpose. Repeat this practice; keep asking the questions and recording the answers. Watch for signals and synchronicities. Read your journal or listen to your recordings, and you will begin to catch the thread of your story—your true destiny.

Consciously pay attention to your thoughts, feelings, and emotions. Are you trying "too hard?" Are you acting out of "shoulds" or what someone else wants you to do? This is a clue that you may be looking for outer rewards. Are you following your bliss? Are you honoring the Self?

A Vision Quest

For millennia, native people have discovered their soul's purpose by going on a vision quest and asking for guidance. If you want to seek your true mission by taking a few days alone in nature, the following are the essentials of this rite of passage:

- Prepare by setting your intention and asking for clarity and protection.
- Separate yourself from your community and your accustomed role.
- Place yourself in a situation of uncertainty and physical deprivation.
- Listen to your inner voice and follow this guidance.

You might go on an organized vision quest with an experienced guide, or you may prefer to retreat by yourself. You might go camping or stay in a cabin in nature for several days. You will want to be alone. Take a journal with you to record your dreams, insights, and revelations—but spend most of your time in silence, meditation, and contemplation. Eat lightly or fast and drink lots of pure water. If you listen within, the answers will come. ("Ask and you shall receive." "Knock and the door will be opened unto you.")

If you have a sense of true purpose, you might use this time to reflect on who your co-creative partners might be. Who are you drawn to work with? Who has gifts and talents that complement yours? Is it time to move into a new Co-creative Core Group, so that you can fully express your potential?

Create a Dream Board

What would your life look like if you were fully living your destiny? Create a "Treasure Map" or "Dream Board," using a piece of poster board. Cut pictures and inspiring words from magazines and paste them onto your board, creating the picture and design of the life you wish to live. Place this where you can see it every day and add to it as you feel so moved.

Creating Space for Your True Mission

Take an inventory of your life. What do you need to let go of to make space for your mission to unfold? What inauthentic activities do you need to release? What internalized teachings, beliefs, and expectations must be liberated to make way for your individual calling? Reflect on these questions and act on your answers.

The following is a useful ritual to release that which no longer serves you. It can be very powerful when done as a group, or you may wish to do it privately at home or in a special place in nature: *Create a sacred space by lighting a candle or burning incense. Write down what you want to release on a piece of paper, and either burn the paper or tear the paper into small pieces and bury them in the Earth. Clarity, focus, and intention will support you in letting go of that which you want to release at this time.*

Evolving Your Work Situation

Often it is appropriate to stay where you are and transform your current relationships or organizations. As well as exploring alternatives outside of your current job, perhaps you can be creative where you are now. You can seek out others in your workplace who may have similar desires. For example, if you are a manager, perhaps you can share co-creative principles with your staff, which ultimately would positively affect all their relationships.

Wherever you are actualizing yourself and empowering others, you are on the front lines of evolution. Ask your Core Group members to help you get ideas about how to evolve and transform your current work situation. Clarify that you are staying in your current job out of choice and attraction, not out of fear.

Coaches, Family, Friends, Mentors

As you explore your life purpose, consult with those who love and know you well. Choose people who will give you loving encouragement rather than negative advice. Seek out supportive, like-minded people. Nurture and protect your new "baby ideas" until they are ready to stand on their own. Emerging ideas and inspirations are delicate and require tender loving care.

When you have a clear idea of your true purpose, look for exemplary models from whom you can learn. Ask for their advice and coaching. Apprentice with them, if appropriate. Deepen your knowledge. Become a student again.

> *Whatever you are born with is God's gift to you.*
> *What you become, is your gift to God.*
>
> *ANONYMOUS*

Fulfilling Your Shared Destiny

When we come together and pool our talents in co-creative collaboration,
a new form of sacredness emerges, one that can truly bless and heal our world.

DAVID SPANGLER

The real leadership that matters is actually the leadership of groups.
The day of the "individual" hero-leader is past. . . We don't need better heroes now,
we need groups of people who can lead—groups of people who can walk ahead.

PETER SENGE

When people come together out of genuine Self interest,
willing to share their strengths and to create a shared vision,
magic happens, synchronicities abound and doors open.
Life naturally evolves out of the chaotic and disorderly,
to a higher level of organization.

JAMES REDFIELD

Teamwork makes the dream work!

SOCIAL ACTIVIST ON TWITTER

*The magnetic energy of the universe that has been forming whole systems for billions
of years—attracting atom to atom, molecule to molecule, and cell to cell—
is joining human to human, creating the nucleus of a new society.*

*The seeds of our individual potentials grow to full stature in the resonant field.
We fulfill our soul's purpose by joining our genius with the genius of others.
This "fusion of genius" unlocks a force as powerful as nuclear fusion:
human creativity.*

*We experience the binding force of universal evolution activating our systems.
The creation that results can be as different and unpredictable
from its source as a child is from his or her parents.*

*We take a quantum leap beyond the capacities of the individuals alone.
Social synergy creates a whole greater than the sum of its parts.
We experience a jump in consciousness, freedom, and creativity.*

*The path to self-actualization in this new cycle of life is co-creation.
With clear guidance and synergy, we can create
what is beyond anything we could do alone.
We are liberated to align with others for the betterment of all.*

Fulfilling Your Shared Destiny

---◆---

From Resonant Core Group to Co-Creative Core Group

ONCE WE HAVE identified our unique life purpose, our natural impulse is to join with others to fulfill our shared destiny. Through a process of discernment, we make new connections and experience how our unique gifts and talents fit into the larger whole. We discover that *all* of our contributions are needed and that the empowerment of one supports the empowerment of all.

We sense that each of us is a cell in the planetary body. We move to the cutting edge of social change, co-creating new structures that enhance synergy and cooperation. We shift from the dominator model of hierarchy and bureaucracy to non-coercive alignment in the partnership model. We link with our peers to create a fully-functioning whole system. A new awareness emerges as we move from self-centered to whole-centered consciousness.

Typically, as we begin to explore our shared destiny, we differentiate from our original Resonant Core. We seek our ideal teammates, reaching out to and attracting those whose purpose is aligned with our own. In this movement from the Resonant Core to a Co-creative Core, our personal growth is enhanced as our focus shifts to include social action or collective expression. Having attained greater spiritual-psychological maturity as the Essential Self, we gradually release the perceived need of the separate self to feel special and central, as we move together into fuller expression. We learn to maintain resonance with our new teammates and turn our attention to expressing our collective genius in the world.

We discover that just as a whole person is balanced spiritually, emotionally, mentally, and physically—these qualities must be present in our Co-creative Core or we will revert back to a dominator structure or fail to model true partnership and mutual empowerment.

In a space of shared Self-actualization, all members of the Core can express their unique talents. If anyone feels unexpressed, we sense it very quickly, as the dissonance diminishes the effectiveness of the team. This critical cross-over point from inner to outer work can be a delicate moment in the life of the Core Group. As the members of the circle differentiate into new Cores, it is vital to continue maintaining resonance and honoring the unique contribution of each person so that the new team can become operative and effective in the world. Patience may be required. It is wise to bond and align with one another before taking action.

The co-creative practices that are offered in Circle 2, Creating and Maintaining Resonance, can be very helpful in building trust and deepening heart connections in the newly-formed Co-creative Core.

The successful group models each part of a loving body—doing what it does best, effortlessly and joyfully, with little or no supervision or external direction. By becoming experienced in the practice of inner listening, everyone knows what to do, moment by moment. Guidance comes from within the individual or from the collective intelligence of the group. If management and coordination are needed, it is gentle and empowering. Needs are met and discord is cleared quickly. The process of decision making shifts as individuals release their egoic need to direct or control and learn to tune into the coherent field of group genius and to discern "what wants to happen." In an ideal environment of creativity and love, synergy occurs. Projects are completed harmoniously and each participant feels energized and fulfilled. *This is the essence of co-creation and the best that it offers.*

The first step in discovering shared destiny is to identify the vision and purpose that embodies the deeper callings and chosen functions of each group member. When you join out of the desire to express your highest potential—the force of creation moves through you, bringing your ideas into alignment and your vision into reality. Your passion is the fuel that fulfills the mission.

In this Circle, you will "heart-storm" a variety of ideas to identify the joint actions that will express your shared purpose and empower you to live your unique potential. You will co-create a Success Statement, succinctly stating your shared vision, mission, and plan of action, as a guide that will support you to do your part in evolving yourselves and society. Making a commitment to action is what allows your heart to finally say "yes" to your life's purpose. It is also the glue that binds you to your teammates and to the fulfillment of your shared destiny.

The essential elements of co-creation, when practiced in concert with one another, provide a model for social action to spring from inner knowing to outer expression. *Usually spiritual groups work on the inner plane and activists work on social problems of the world. This sourcing of social action from within brings these together and is a key to peaceful personal and planetary transformation! This joining of Essence and action defines the unique power of co-creation.*

The dominant culture that currently prevents natural synergy by utilizing social structures which accentuate separation, create forced ranking, and suppress empathy and creativity is gradually giving way to the new model of co-creation: self-governance by attunement to the universal pattern within each person and through alignment with others and with the natural world.

Guided Meditation: Aligning in Shared Purpose

The purpose of this meditation is to allow you to experience what it might feel like to join your purpose and genius with that of your ideal co-creative partners. The facilitator slowly reads this aloud, remembering to pause between phrases. If you prefer, you can play the recording of this meditation—available online at www.cocreatorshandbook.com.

Close your eyes and take some deep breaths, inviting your body to relax . . . Feel your heart opening more fully.

(Pause)

Evoke a feeling of gratitude for the circumstances of your life and for the gifts of inner peace and creative expression . . . Feel your energy expanding and merging with the energies of all the others in this circle and with all life.

(Pause for 1 minute)

Now, envision yourself in nature, standing before a pool of water . . . It is deep and clear. . . Engage all your senses as you take a moment to enjoy the sights, smells, and sounds that surround this beautiful pool.

(Pause)

As you focus on the surface of the pool, forms slowly take shape . . . First, you see the image of Canada geese in flight—in a perfect "V" formation . . . Notice how perfectly aligned they are with one another . . . gliding effortlessly above the water.

(Pause for 1 minute)

Now, visualize a hive of bees . . . Notice how they work as a team, collecting pollen and making honey in cooperation with one another.

(Pause for 1 minute)

Next, bring into your awareness a gorgeous red rose . . . each petal embracing the surrounding petals . . . each petal contributing its beauty to the perfection and magnificence of the whole.

(Pause for 1 minute)

Allow yourself to appreciate fully the natural order, harmony, and unity that exist all around you.

(Pause)

Mentally gaze again into the water of the pool . . . In the depths of the water envision people all over the world cooperating with nature and with one another . . . As best you are able, feel yourself aligning your unique gifts and talents with your ideal teammates, co-creating with others in complete harmony . . . How does this feel?

(Pause for 1 minute)

Focus your attention on each of the people presently gathered in this circle and acknowledge their light, their love, and their unique gifts . . . See your light joining with theirs, creating a great glowing orb of light.

(Pause for 1 minute)

Now expand this light and imagine that all members of the human family are expressing their full potential . . . Envision society as one coordinated body . . . every function evolving as a part of a whole.

(Pause for 1 minute)

Now, slowly become aware once again of your surroundings . . . Sense your presence in this room . . . Slowly move your hands and feet . . . When you are ready, open your eyes and take in the beauty of each person in the circle.

As you "Check In" at the beginning of this meeting, share your experience of this meditation with the other members of your group.

Essential Elements of a Co-Creative Core

A co-creative team models balance, coherence, and wholeness. The group may consist of as few as two people or as many as 12 or more; however, in order to model co-creation at least one or more team members must be able to hold the vision, maintain resonance, set up systems and structures, and carry out the required action.

Vision is the spiritual component of the project or activity; resonance is the emotional ingredient; systems and structures are expressions of mental acuity; and implementation is the physical aspect of any venture. *If any of these elements are missing, the team cannot succeed in modeling co-creation. A team may be able to complete their project or program, but the process used will not have been co-creative and will fall short of its greater potential.*

It is important to bear this in mind as you attract your ideal teammates. Before you agree to work together, each member can ask herself:

> *"What are my personal strengths?"*
> *"Am I a visionary?"*
> *"Do I have an ability to set up systems to support effective action?"*
> *"Do I naturally emanate love and empathy?" ("Am I what Eckhart Tolle calls a 'frequency holder'?")*
> *"Do I gain satisfaction from completing projects and producing results?"*

Share your insights with one another. After making these determinations, be sure that all four capacities are present in your group, even if there are only two of you on your team. If any one of these capacities is missing in your group, become proactive to attract and engage at least one additional resonant person who embodies the function that is missing.

Defining Shared Purpose

———————— ❧ ————————

DISCUSS THE FOLLOWING ideas and principles. If you wish, co-create any other principles that reflect your understanding and experience of collaborating consciously with others.

- Shared purpose is never manufactured or artificially imposed; rather it emerges from the life purposes and collective visions of its members. Just notice what is real for each of you. Ask yourself, "What do I feel aligned with at the level of my soul?" "What is worth doing?" "What project or social issue has true value for me?"
- To have members support a purpose, the purpose must support them! In order to sustain interest and commitment, the shared purpose must result in some personal rewards for each group member: meeting new people, personal growth, self-actualization, satisfaction from contributing, acquiring new skills, compensation, etc.
- Be sure the joint project or group focus draws forth the creativity of ALL of its members. Each person must be authentic to their soul's purpose.
- The value of partnership and teamwork without competition must be understood. The gifts of all members are necessary to actualize shared destiny.
- Manifestation comes from forces that are totally aligned and integrated. Therefore, the group focus must be sustainable, there must be resonance, and the vision must be held by all.
- Shared purpose is a serious commitment to action and requires the loyalty of each group member to fulfill his agreements to the project or vision. There is a morality in co-creation to care for and nurture the work. Promising to do projects with people and then not following through will not work. This can destroy trust in a group and sabotage your joint project.
- Know that the process of creating shared purpose may be a transformational end in itself. It is not necessary to force an intended result. Follow your guidance and allow the project to unfold organically.

Tips for Actualizing Shared Purpose

———— ❧ ————

READ THROUGH THE following tips; then discuss and modify them to reflect your knowing and experience. Much of what is presented here is a recap of the work you have already done in your circle. In your next exercise you will be putting these principles into action as you create your Success Statement.

- Using the power of synergy, the group accesses inner knowing and translates the life calling of each member and shared purpose of the group into a collective plan of action.
- Each person sources the plan or project, bringing it forth from the depth of his co-creative being. People are not helping out one key leader, but rather fulfilling their unique purposes together. Partnership and cooperation prevail, with the goal of overall group empowerment.
- Each member takes full responsibility for her part as well as for the whole. It is important to recognize the interdependence of members in the group rather than to operate from dependent, independent, or enabling behaviors.
- Individuals live as their word, clearly communicating their promises and keeping their agreements. If you break your word or make a mistake, you self correct. If someone else makes a mistake, you gently offer feedback with discernment and without condemnation. Positive and negative feedback are given easily with no one protected from knowing the truth. Self-governance emerges naturally within a mature group.
- The authority of knowing prevails. "Sapiential authority" means that the one who is most adept leads during the activity when his knowledge is of prime importance. This requires group trust and empowerment. In situations where there is no particular authority needed, collective guidance prevails.
- Alignment takes the place of regimentation. If individuals are centered and actualizing their soul's purpose, they will naturally align with others doing the same. Alignment is experienced as deep, spontaneous agreement, reinforcement, trust, encouragement, and love. It makes work a joy and transforms the workplace from an arena of effort into an oasis of creativity and cooperation.
- Natural leadership is given to those who intuitively know how to empower others for the good of the whole. People who are natural synergistic leaders may not have been

able to succeed in manipulative or competitive settings. Every group should be alert to those who have a gift of focalizing, facilitating, and bringing the best out in everyone.

- Everyone aims at win/win solutions. There can be no real win if someone has lost. In a Co-creative Core Group, each member is touched by the experiences of others. The group functions as one body.

- Any competition is transformed in community through shared purpose. All functions are equally important to fully manifest the group vision.

- Once action begins, the group needs some sense of order. It is helpful to select a coordinator or coordinators to maintain focus, track results, and serve as a communication link between members of the group. This management is guided by the policies of the whole, yet is given authority to direct the parts as needed.

- Communication is key to maintaining a resonant field of trust and cooperation. Keep members of the group informed about any progress as well as setbacks. Re-create resonance and alignment as necessary.

- Clear out any fears, resistances, and limiting beliefs which may defeat your purpose and sabotage your results.

- Group members are committed to practicing all the Circles of Co-Creation as they engage with their purpose in the world—especially the practices of resonance, inspired insights, and clearing. The process and the end results become one in a co-creative culture. By modeling that change ourselves, we do in fact change the world.

Co-creating Your Success Statement

———————— ❈ ————————

A FUNCTIONAL TEAM is one in which the participants are energized and empowered. It consists of the right people in the right place at the right time doing what they enjoy and fulfilling their unique callings.

The right people for a team are those who are aligned with the purpose; have a natural affinity for one another; trust one another's intentions, integrity, and competence; have the skills needed; want to participate; and are willing to take action. In other words, they are able to see the vision, are clear about its mission, feel passionate about the project, and are committed to achieving its intended results. When people do what they enjoy, they are enthusiastic and inspired and are able to accomplish remarkable results effortlessly!

Whether you are considering a one-time community project, enhancing your existing work situation, or starting a new business—you will need to identify your shared vision, mission, and action to achieve your purpose. These components or steps comprise what we call a Success Statement and are some of the main practices described in this chapter. If your team is willing to move consciously through this process together, you will have laid the foundation for a successful program or business.

Be sure to allow ample time. Depending on the complexity of your project, you may need several half-day meetings or one-day sessions to complete all the processes in this chapter with your prospective co-creators. Do not rush these steps. Before beginning, be sure that you have materials to record your insights and proceedings. You might want to record the entire session to transcribe it later, or you might appoint a scribe. Also, you will want to have your own computer or journal and pen handy to keep track of personal insights. Use a computer, flip chart, or large sheets of paper and marker pens to record ideas shared with the group. *Read the entire set of processes through before planning your meetings and choose the appropriate meeting formats for your situation.*

Clarity and honesty are important at this stage. A Success Statement must emerge from the life purposes and collective visions of *every* member of your group.

Step 1. Defining Your Vision

Vision is the expression of Spirit on the material plane. It is an expansive, idealistic perception of what is possible to bring forth in the human experience. It is a passionate expression of your dream. A true vision statement inspires and uplifts; it touches your heart and expands your awareness.

THE PROCESS

- Have ready access to your computer or to a pen and paper before you begin.
- Center yourselves with a few moments of silence. Feel your connection to one another as one body in deep resonance.
- When you feel in tune with one another, the facilitator asks these questions: "What is your vision for yourself, and what is your vision for this group?"
- Spend a few minutes in silence, listening carefully to your inner voice and being aware of any images that come to you. "Reach for the stars" and do not edit or limit what comes to you in any way.
- As you get insights or images, write them down. Begin your entries with the words:

    My vision for myself is ...
    My vision for this group is ...

- When all of you have completed this process, share your vision with each other.
- If you prefer, you can use an inspired insights process to discover the group vision. In this case, when the facilitator asks, "What is your vision for this group?" you would answer out loud as you feel moved to respond. Remember to record this process or have one member of your group write down the insights.

- Regardless of which approach you have used to access your group vision, ask yourself: "Do I feel expanded by these words?" "Does this vision touch my heart and lift my spirit?" "Do I resonate fully with these words and this feeling tone?"
- Once you have aligned around your shared vision, *create a brief written statement that clearly communicates your dream of what is possible.*

Step 2: Clarifying Your Mission

Your mission defines what you intend to accomplish with regard to the vision. It describes the purpose for which your service, project, or business exists. It activates and aligns the purpose of each member of your group, putting your individual callings into practice. Often, just a few words can describe the essence of your project or business. (For example, the slogan of FedEx is: "The World on Time.") Just as your vision statement is the spiritual component of your plan, your mission statement is the mental component. *Its keynote is clarity.* Try to keep your mission statement concise and powerful.

From your mission you derive your goals, objectives, and detailed action plan. A mission statement combines rational thinking and intuitive knowing and provides focused, specific, and clear information about how you will accomplish your vision. It points to why your project or business exists.

THE PROCESS
Read through the instructions before you begin.

- Make sure you feel centered, peaceful, and relaxed by taking a few minutes to attune and connect with one another. You might listen to a piece of beautiful music, create a guided visualization, or be with one another in silence for a few minutes.
- The facilitator asks the following questions, allowing time for you to respond to each one and to record your answers:

    What is our mission?
    What project is calling us as a group?

Why is it important?
How does our group mission relate to your personal passion, gifts, and life purpose?

- Now, the facilitator says, *Allow any questions that you have about the group mission to surface. Ask your questions out loud as they come to you. Respond verbally to others' questions from a place of deep centeredness.*
- When everyone has had an opportunity to express themselves, the facilitator will invite the group to gently open their eyes and share what they have discovered in this process.

Step 3. Refining Your Mission Statement

THE PROCESS

- Your next step is to *refine* your mission statement and align on the precise words that reflect the essence of your work together. One of you can act as the scribe to write all the proposed mission statements on a flip chart or on large sheets of paper. From all the suggested phrases, co-create the one statement that most precisely reflects your shared purpose. It's important that each member of your Core feels aligned with the statement.
- This is not a time for compromise! Be sure that your written statement clearly communicates your aligned purpose. Every substantive word should be meaningful for each of you! Remember: vision inspires and mission informs. Your individual and shared passion will move the mission and vision forward.
- When you have completed this portion of your Success Statement, reflect on these questions: Do you love what it says? Does your vision statement uplift you? Is your mission statement clear and informative? If you plan to create a website, your vision and mission statements will be posted prominently there for the world to see!
- The next time you come back together, do a centering process and read your Statement aloud as a way to align your group. Let the essence of the words reach deeply into your

hearts and minds. Share your passion and any insights you have about it with each other and, if you all agree, make any modifications. Begin your future gatherings with this procedure. (You will complete your Success Statement at your next session, when you add your actions.)

Moving into Aligned Action

Step 4. Identifying the Actions to Fulfill Your Mission

AT THIS POINT, most of you probably already have one or more notions and strategies about how to accomplish your mission. Use those ideas to launch a creative "heartstorming" session. Heartstorming—tuning into the intelligence of your heart—in addition to brainstorming, allows you to release valuable ideas that might be judged by the mind as unworthy, inefficient, impossible, or extravagant. Ultimately, your plan should be action oriented and include specific tasks and "due dates." It will also identify who is responsible for performing each function.

Your action steps are the physical component of your plan, and your passion is the emotional factor that provides the juice, driving your project to successful fulfillment.

You will need more than two people to do this process. If your group is small, ask other friends or colleagues who share interest in your project to join you. Sometimes it is valuable to ask someone who is resonant, but not familiar with what you are doing, to participate in your heartstorming session. You may find that they bring interesting perspectives that you may not have considered.

Prepare for your session by having a computer, flip chart, or large sheets of paper and markers available. Select a scribe to capture all of your ideas. You also may want to record the session so you can refer to it later. This is a time for creative expression and not a time for discussion or analysis.

THE PROCESS

- Begin with a centering process or visualization.
- The facilitator poses these questions, pausing between each one to invite insights to emerge:

> *What are all the ways we can think of to achieve our mission?*
> *What are our ideas regarding our possible actions?*
> *What strategies are most appropriate?*

185

- From a quiet centered state, share your inspired insights as they arise.
- Let the ideas flow. The scribe writes down all the ideas for everyone to see. The pace may be fast—idea followed by idea.
- You will know your session is over when no new ideas are flowing. When that happens, it might be a good time to take a break. If you take a break, center yourselves again when you reconvene. Then continue the process.
- Look at your list of possible actions and strategies.
- Create a list of the most important criteria for the joint actions you will choose to undertake. Examples of criteria might be: most likely to be accomplished within a reasonable time frame; most enjoyable; least effort for the greatest results; serves the largest audience (customers and/or constituents); adds the most value; has the greatest potential for generating revenue; this team has the needed expertise.
- Remember to tune into the field of collective intelligence and to balance your rational analysis with your intuitive knowing.
- Look at both the action ideas and strategies and the most important criteria for action lists. Then, in the margin beside each criterion on the list, write down the number(s) of the action ideas that you feel best meet that criterion.
- Discuss your responses. Identify the ideas that best match your criteria for successful joint action. For each one, ask the following question: *Is this idea for action likely to fulfill our mission, and is it aligned with our values and vision?*

Once you have completed this round, for each action item ask the following question: *What obstacle(s) might impede or hinder us from fulfilling this action?* Have the scribe note any perceived obstacles or challenges. Then discuss how you might overcome these obstacles. Again, allow time for solitude to reflect on the results of these processes. At your next meeting or after a break, align behind your top actions.

Note: There are many techniques besides heartstorming for bringing forth creative ideas. One of these is "mind mapping," in which ideas generated by the group are connected with lines to other ideas. Software is available to assist with this nonlinear process.

Finally, write a statement that accurately reflects your chosen actions. Be sure to estimate the cost and time frame for each item. Use the same procedure you used for writing your mission statement. An action statement is concrete and clear. It reflects the specific steps you will take to fulfill your mission.

Finally, read your entire Success Statement: Vision, Mission, and Action and celebrate your alignment. Acknowledge the passion you feel for this. You have just completed a process that can lay a strong foundation for the success of your project or business!

Ceremony: Aligning in Shared Purpose

After you have created your Success Statement, honor this achievement by aligning in shared purpose through ceremony.

Stand in a circle together. One person begins by moving to the center of the circle and clearly stating her soul's purpose. She then shares what is most needed at this time to fulfill her purpose. (people, resources, prayers, logistical support, etc.) Another person, who feels that she can offer support, steps into the circle and takes her hand. This second person then states her life purpose and offers her specific support. The process continues as each person, one by one, joins hands with another, states her unique purpose and offers support.

When each person has stepped forward, take a few moments to observe the web of connections that are naturally interwoven as you give your unique gifts in service to the whole. Be seated again and share any additional insights. Acknowledge the connections and the empowerment that is available as the self-organizing process supports your needs and brings your group into coherence and shared purpose.

Review the Co-Creator's Agreements

If your group has not reviewed the Co-Creator's Agreements recently, do that now. Are there any changes you wish to make at this time? These guiding principles reflect your values and are central to the actions you will be taking to fulfill your shared destiny.

Acknowledge Your Commitment

When you are clear about your shared purpose and satisfied with the functions each of you will fulfill in the joint action(s), you *will be* committed. So, rather than feeling the need to "make" a commitment, simply notice if you are, indeed, committed! Your dedication to the team and your plan of action will be firm as long as they continue to fulfill your shared purpose and personal calling.

Attraction is the key. Notice if you feel passion for the mission and resonance with your co-creative partners. If you are not fully committed, clarify what is uncomfortable for you. "Making" a commitment at this point will only overshadow whatever needs to be addressed for you to be truly committed.

If you wish, this might be a good time to celebrate your commitment to the fulfillment of your shared purpose. Refer to the Ceremony of Commitment in Circle 5.

Until one is committed, there is hesitancy, the chance to draw back,
always ineffectiveness. Concerning all acts of initiative (and creation),
there is one elementary truth the ignorance of which kills countless ideas and
splendid plans: the moment one definitely commits oneself, then Providence moves too.

All sorts of things occur to help one that would never otherwise have occurred.
A whole stream of events issues from the decision, raising in one's favor
all manner of unforeseen incidents and meetings and material assistance,
which no man could have dreamed would have come his way.

I have learned a deep respect for one of Goethe's couplets:
"Whatever you can do, or dream you can, begin it.
Boldness has genius, power and magic in it!"

W.N. Murray

Deepening Practice

Following is an exercise to be done on your own.

Review Your Success Statement

ONCE YOUR GROUP has completed your Success Statement, take time to reflect on each element. Do you feel deeply aligned with the vision and mission? Do you resonate with the action steps? Do you intuit how this project is empowering and in harmony with your unique calling? How does this Success Statement feel in your body? Are there any changes you would make?

Write down any insights in your journal and share these with your team when you next meet. Be open to making any adjustments to your Success Statement, if any changes have surfaced since your group last met together. As you evolve as a team, your Statement will evolve.

Attuning to the Design of Creation

*There is a new way of operating and it is not really about making
this decision or that decision, the right decision or the
wrong decision. It is more like navigating a flow.
You feel where events are moving, and you feel for the right thing to do.
It's like a river that knows which way to turn
around a rock—to the left or to the right.
It's an intuitive and innate sense of knowing.*

ADYASHANTI

*We must enter new territory and immerse our whole being, our whole mind
and spirit in a very different paradigm and perceptual experience.
We must develop the skill of intentionally altering perception and thinking
to solve the problems that older kinds of thinking have caused.
It is an evolutionary necessity.*

STEPHEN HARROD BUHNER

*There is no logical way to the discovery of elemental laws.
There is only the way of intuition, which is helped by a feeling
for the order lying behind appearance.*

ALBERT EINSTEIN.

Michelangelo released the magnificent figures he saw encased in stone;
he did not make them. So it is with all co-creation—decisions among them.

Decisions are "tapping into the universal design" to notice how
the pattern unfolds in the great tapestry of life.

They are derived from tuning into "what wants to happen"
and right relations. They are guided by love rather than driven by fear.
Decision making thus becomes "releasing the decision" by discovering the
natural design of creation, the Tao of right action.

We join together and allow a fuller understanding
of the greater picture to emerge.

We move by inspiration rather than obligation
and discover what most naturally wants to occur with ease and grace.
All are empowered as we collectively access and co-evolve the inherent design.

True self-governance arises as we join with others and attune
to the universal pattern which lives within each of us,
expressed as our unique purpose
and released through co-creative decision making.

Attuning to the Design of Creation

IT IS OBVIOUS that our current institutions no longer meet the needs of our evolving humanity. A top down approach does not work for a living organism, such as a team of people. Hierarchical structures stifle creativity and suppress the soul. Individuals and groups are seeking the freedom to respond to issues based on their own intuition and ability to attune to a higher order. As we evolve, we stabilize as our Essential Selves and learn to govern ourselves for the good of all.

Our internal guidance directs us to birth whole systems and new structures that express our values and support the fulfillment of our individual and shared destiny. We acknowledge the self-organizing principle of nature as we explore new possibilities and create innovative forms of governance which reflect our basic character as integral expressions of the universal pattern of creation.

In this Circle we explore what it means to operate from a whole systems perspective and to practice self-governance. As we attune to the design of creation, we naturally desire to make optimum choices which honor our interconnectedness with all life. We evolve beyond linear thinking, majority rule, and consensus decision making and enter into a practice of aligning consciously with "the pattern that connects" to determine what wants to happen moment by moment. We affirm that what appears to be chaotic, exemplifies order—when seen from a larger perspective.

As we shift from self-centered to whole-centered consciousness, we make choices which honor both the masculine and feminine aspects of our being and our community. We find the right balance between structure and flow. We come to the circle as equals, and all voices are heard and respected. We move beyond control and manipulation and open to trust what naturally wants to emerge in a self-organizing process. Taking the complete picture into account, we release to guidance through the practice of inspired insights.

We are going through an unprecedented planetary transformation in which there are no authorities who can give us the answers. Learning to listen to our inner knowing at this moment of evolutionary change is as vital as learning to read and write. We will not find the answers out there, but must develop the inner tools to discover innovative solutions to the vast challenges that confront us. More than "deciding" what is right action, we become one with the situation and act in a natural flow. Our ultimate goal is for the authority within to prevail and guide us through our transformation from separated individuals to united members of one global family.

Guided Meditation: Attuning to the Design of Creation

The facilitator reads this aloud, remembering to pause between phrases. You may want to play soft, beautiful music in the background. If you prefer, you can play the recording of this guided meditation that is available at www.cocreatorshandbook.com.

Gently close your eyes and take several deep breaths, inviting your body to relax . . . releasing any feelings of tension, any tightness or physical discomfort.

(Pause)

Take another deep breath into your heart and feel the presence of the others in this circle . . . Take a moment to send and receive love from each person who is sharing this meditation.

(Pause)

Be aware of the Earth beneath your feet . . . this beautiful planet that is our home. Tune into the energies of the rocks and minerals, the trees and plants, the animals and insects . . . the profusion of life forms that are connected in an intricate and magnificent web of energy and vitality.

(Pause)

And now turn your attention within . . . Think of a time when you were at an important crossroads in your life and needed to make a choice or a decision that only you could resolve . . . a time when you might have felt torn in two different directions . . . when you felt unclear which way to turn . . . Take a moment to allow any images or sensations to emerge . . . Notice how this memory feels in your body.

(Pause for 1 - 2 minutes)

Is there any emotion attached to this memory? . . . If so, what is that emotion? Once you made a choice, was this decision made from your head? or from your heart? or from your gut? . . . Were you true to yourself?

(Pause for 1 - 2 minutes)

Is there any lesson to be learned from this? . . . Does this decision reveal a pattern of behavior? . . . Does it reflect your ability to tune into what wants to happen in the moment?

(Pause)

Now, as best you are able, let go of these thoughts and focus once again on your radiant heart. Affirm that the source of greatest wisdom lies within . . . not in your head, but in your heart . . . in your body. Know that by making this journey from head to heart, you can access the answer to any problem you may be facing . . . You can attune to the larger pattern of creation and feel into what is right action in each moment.

(Pause)

Place your hand on your heart and anchor this knowing there . . . Affirm silently that you are a unique expression of divine intelligence . . . and that all answers are available to you when you ask and look within.

(Pause)

Tune into a decision that is present in your life at this time . . . Perhaps it is a simple decision or a major one in terms of potential impact on your life. Continue to put attention on your heart and body wisdom . . . Feel into the choices that are in front of you. Focus on one possibility and imagine making this choice . . . How does it feel in your body? Is there a sense of spaciousness and freedom? . . . Or perhaps do you feel a contraction and sense of limitation?

(Pause for 1 minute)

Imagine making another choice and follow the same process of feeling it in your heart and body . . . Is there any experience of fear or do you feel joyful considering this possibility? . . . Take a few moments to go back and forth between these two choices. Do feelings of obligation or guilt arise with either possibility? . . . Notice which choice brings vitality and a sense of aliveness.

(Pause for 1 minute)

As you take another deep breath and release any mental activity as much as possible, feel in your body if you are being true to yourself . . . Are you honoring your whole being: body, heart, mind and Spirit? Allow the decision to easily arise as you relax into your inherent knowing.

(Pause)

Now take another deep breath and sense yourself back in this circle. . . . Be aware of the life force bringing vitality to every cell of your body . . . This is Spirit expressing through physical form. When you are ready, open your eyes, and connect visually with the others in your circle.

Before checking in with your circle, create a dyad or triad and share your experience of this meditation with one another. What insights have come to you? If you wish, capture these insights in your journal.

Check-in

Re-read together the introductory material for this Circle. As you check in, share what you are feeling as you shift from an old to a new way of being. What are you releasing in your life? What is being born in you? What is your "evolutionary edge?" Discuss how you might support one another at this time.

Co-Creative Decision Making

---❈---

Presence is a state of inner spaciousness.
When you are present, you ask:
How do I respond to the needs of the situation, of this moment?
Look and listen—become one with the situation.
When instead of reacting against a situation, you merge with it,
the solution arises out of the situation itself.
Alert stillness listens. Then, if action is possible or necessary,
you take action or rather right action happens through you.
Right action is action that is appropriate to the whole.

ECKHART TOLLE

OF ALL THE practices that a co-creative team must employ, the one that is often the most challenging is decision making. When we operate in a hierarchical model, decision making is very straight-forward: the boss decides. The people at the top hold the power and determine what direction a project or business will take. In the partnership model, all those who are stakeholders and will be impacted by decisions must either offer their proxy or be consulted or considered in some way. Their interests must be represented and honored.

New challenges may emerge as the team grows. It can be easy for a handful of people to communicate frequently with one another and to align their actions. But what do you do if you are dealing with an entire community or business and a decision might impact all members of this extended team? Is it necessary to consult each person and gain their approval before moving forward? Might small teams be empowered to make decisions for the larger group?

The following chart indicates the distinctions between the decision-making strategies of a hierarchical organization and the process of co-creative organizations of attuning collectively to what wants to emerge.   Discuss these differences with your Core Group and make any additions that feel relevant.

HIERARCHICAL DECISION-MAKING	CO-CREATIVE DECISION-MAKING
Identify a problem or opportunity	Identify a problem or opportunity
Logical	Intuitive
Analytical	Accesses deep knowing
Asks: who has the power to make this happen?	Asks: who would be impacted?
Asks: what are the options?	Asks: what's in the flow?
Asks: what's the logical decision?	Asks: what wants to emerge?
Asks: what are the risks?	Asks: what are the opportunities?
Asks: what benefits us?	Asks: what honors the whole?
Comes from a personal point of view	Transpersonal; divines the design
May result in a win/lose decision	Focuses on a win/win for all
Engages the mind	Engages body, mind, heart and Spirit
Looks to the past	Senses from an emerging future
Operates from habitual patterns	Sees with fresh eyes

Practices that Support Co-Creative Decision Making

We learn to let go and listen to the life that wants to be lived through us....
we shift from external to internal yardsticks in our decision making.
We are now concerned with the question of inner rightness:
does this decision seem right? Am I being true to myself?
Is this in line with who I sense I am called to become?
Am I being of service to the world?

FREDERIC LALOUX

In determining right action, co-creators shift away from linear thinking and traditional decision making practices. We tune into the field, the space between us, and tap into the one consciousness that expresses through many vehicles. Our decisions emerge in this field. It is as though our minds and voices are being orchestrated by being in this space together. We use our non-kinesthetic feeling sense and the wisdom of our hearts to tune into a larger pattern. We are lifted collectively to a higher order and bring into being a transcendent wisdom. With practice, we learn to integrate an entire informational inflow into one holistic gestalt, generating a response that comes out of a unique state of being. We gain the ability to access this collective intelligence through resonance, alignment, and intent. A new state of consciousness gives rise to a practice that honors the whole and liberates our sense of a separate self. We move beyond the thinking mind and consensus to access what wants to emerge in this moment. We experience what it means to "grok" a solution.[4] We divine the design of the movement of life that brings coherence and resolution to the issue at hand.

Discuss

Decision making can become a spiritual practice of deep communion—as we move beyond personal will, align with our individual and shared purpose, tune into the higher pattern of creation, and commit to taking action that serves the good of the whole. Discuss these ideas with your Core Group and add any qualities that seem relevant to you. Later in this chapter, you will be establishing your own set of criteria for decision making. Some of the following qualities may be relevant for your team at that time.

The inherent traits that support what is often called whole systems or co-creative decision making, might be called "attuned alignment practices." They include the following:

- Uniting around a shared intention to resolve the issue effortlessly
- Affirming that for every challenge there are multiple solutions
- Creating a collective agreement field of shared resonance
- Honoring all perspectives by practicing deep listening

---

4 Grok is a word coined by Robert A. Heinlein for his 1961 science-fiction novel *Stranger in a Strange Land*. Grok means "to understand intuitively or by empathy, to establish rapport with, to tune into a pattern or gestalt."

- Releasing preconceived notions, attachments, judgments, and positionality
- Acknowledging that there is a divine design that can be accessed when we tune in
- Realizing that there is no need to convert, fix, or change anyone
- Placing our attention on the whole, rather than on the particular
- When appropriate, empowering a smaller team to decide for the group
- Balancing efficiency, streamlining the process, and honoring the group principles
- Allowing decisions to emerge that are congruent with the group's values and inner knowing
- Being actively engaged in the process and taking full responsibility and ownership for the decision

Principles of Co-Creative or Whole Systems Decision Making

*Whole systems decision-making is a practice through which we apprentice
our awareness, in a group context, to the aspect of the divine
which choreographs the dance of life. It is an advanced spiritual practice of attunement in the divine activity. Among other things, we complete
our learning of how choice and effect operate by recognizing the
consequences of our choices as they ripple in both directions—
into our inner world and our outer world.
When we reach this condition of attunement with the self-organizing dance,
we meet in a place where choice and no choice converge.
It is place of synthesis unity where the awareness of right relation and
right timing is so clear that we would consider no other choice
than being in optimal relationship with all.*

RICH RUSTER

TAKE TIME IN your group to read and talk about the following principles of whole system's decision making. Share examples of how you have or could use these principles when making decisions or working with issues. Affirm for yourselves that these principles are aligned with your
knowing and experience. Remember that, like other evolutionary processes, co-creative decision
making is not a linear process. It involves principles to be practiced in concert with one another.

Individuals who operate at the level of Second-tier (in the Spiral Dynamics model) are naturally attracted to whole systems decision making. It is the state of consciousness from which
these practices emerge.

1. Honor Body, Mind, and Spirit
The value of what is often called the linear, left-side of the brain or masculine way of processing information is greatly enhanced when used in concert with your artistic, intuitive, more

feminine way of knowing. Learning to honor and draw upon both aspects of your mind creates a "whole brain approach" to accessing clarity. It is an expansion from linear to holographic thinking.

Your cognitive mind helps you to collect, categorize, classify, analyze, and synthesize data. Your intuition allows you to access your higher mind, heart wisdom, and somatic intelligence.

Be mindful of the messages being transmitted by your body—which sometimes can be expressed through tension, pain, or discomfort. Bodies are inherently wise and often hold the necessary information to make a whole systems decision.

2. Observe What is Naturally Occurring

In a self-organizing system, decisions are revealed by observing what is naturally occurring. Become one with the situation, paying careful attention to where energy is moving and then articulate the process. Release the need to control and predict by trusting life's ability to self-organize. Through this recognition, you can identify new forms and structures that are in alignment with a higher consciousness. Often a decision has already emerged and the answer is patently obvious.

3. Align with Nature and Natural Law

Align powerfully with your intention; nature will provide the energy to guide you in your actions. You will experience alignment as deep spontaneous agreement, synchronicity, reinforcement, trust, encouragement, and love. Be silent and ask that the larger pattern be revealed.

4. Focus on Internal Values

The internal process and the path you take to achieve your goals should be consistent. Are you currently modeling the result you want? Are your values embodied in your actions? Plant the seeds in the present moment that are fully aligned with your intent, purpose, and objectives. Be accountable to your internal process. Learn to govern from the inside out and to follow the promptings of Spirit.

5. Relax and Have Fun; Invite Decisions to be Revealed with Ease

Have you ever had a word "on the tip of your tongue"? Have you noticed that the harder you try to remember it, the more difficult it is? Finally, you let it go and move on to something else. In a flash the word appears!

So much brilliance emerges when you are taking a walk, having a shower, or awakening in the middle of the night. The state of resonance is a relaxed state. From this state you can release what you already know. Often when you think it is time to buckle down and get to work, it is when you most need to lighten up and relax! You will discover that many decisions reveal themselves when you are taking a break!

6. Those Who Know, Lead

Leadership is a reflection of the consciousness and connection of the group and mirrors the highest purpose to which the group aspires. Leadership naturally flows from member to member as the focus of the group changes. In order for true growth to occur, the leadership must be open and flexible. Each individual, through his inner guidance, offers his unique talents and insights in response to the needs of the moment. Therefore, the leadership rotates as the individual with the greatest knowing steps forward to lead.

7. Empower One Another

In dominator models of social organization, power is understood as taking and holding on to control. To maintain status or to prevent being left out, people may feel that they have to do things which are not their natural gifts.

In contrast, in whole systems or co-creative decision making, you discover who has the best knowledge for each activity and then you empower each other to do what you do best. In a co-creative society, power is what you each exhibit when you are in your element—when it is clear you know what to do. You "give away your power" when you do not step forward with your unique gifts and do not share what you know at the appropriate time.

8. Form New Structures that Support Empowerment and Equality

The old forms of domination and submission were characterized by force, coercion, control, and fear. It is no wonder that the old form of deciding was conducted in organizations that had "divisions" (cut off from others) and "departments" (boxed in). By accentuating separation and suppressing empathy and creativity, these structures prevented natural synergy.

In co-creative decision making, each part contributes its precise function freely as a cell within a living body. Each person is honored and respected for his unique gifts. Moving beyond perceptions of scarcity and competition, co-creators build new structures and protocols based on abundance and cooperation. The circle is one of these structures that fosters creative expression and empowers all members of a team. Shared purpose and appreciation for each individual's unique contributions lead to positive change and expansion.

9. Suspend Judgments and be Aware of Habitual Ways of Thinking

To tap into "what wants to happen," it is essential to suspend judgments, abandon certainty, let go of the need to know or to control the outcome, and approach each decision with "beginner's mind." Pay attention to unexamined assumptions, those unconscious habits or thought forms that can misdirect or block a decision from being revealed. It works best if each participant in the attunement process is not attached to outcome and can maintains awareness of his personal beliefs and patterns of thinking, without imposing those on the group.

10. Honor the Self as You Focus on the Whole

A key to releasing the best decisions is to acknowledge that each person is responsible for her own needs. Assessing what is right for you and communicating clearly is the responsibility of each member of the Co-creative Core.

In co-creative organizations everyone's needs are considered and there is always a decision that supports the whole. Allow enough time for reflection as you approach decision making and track that all voices have been heard or represented. Check in with the group to be sure that there is collective ownership of the decision, once it has emerged.

11. Communicate with Integrity

While engaged in this practice, consider whether what you are about to say moves the process forward or stops the flow. If it may stop the flow, rephrase it before speaking. Communicate your truth, clearly and without drama. As best you are able, see with fresh eyes and take responsibility for your emotions by being authentic and appropriate in your expression.

12. Go with the Flow

If you notice undue struggle, effort, or drama in arriving at a decision, take time to re-establish your relationships with each other and align behind your mission. There may be underlying emotions, a lack of resonance, unquestioned beliefs, or issues of control. You may want to refer to the processes for overcoming feelings of separation in Circle 3.

Proceed only when you feel totally aligned again. This may necessitate taking a break and reassembling at a later time or letting the issue rest for a while. Sometimes it is not "right timing" for a decision to be revealed. Perhaps other insights or additional information is needed. Trust the process. When the time is right, the appropriate next steps will emerge with ease.

13. A Final Question

Before proceeding with your final decision, ask yourselves, *"What would LOVE do?"*

Practicing Co-Creative Decision Making

Where there is no hierarchy of bosses over subordinates,
space becomes available for other natural and spontaneous hierarchies
to spring up—fluid hierarchies of recognition, influence, and skill (sometime referred
to as "actualization hierarchies" in place of traditional
"dominator hierarchies.")

Frederic Laloux

In a sense, there's no decision making. What to do just becomes obvious.
You can't rush it. You need to 'feel out' what to do. You hang back, you observe.
You don't act out of deduction, you act out of an inner feeling,
making sense as you go. You're not even thinking.
You're at one with the situation.

Brian Arthur

As you have probably experienced, in a resonant group setting we gain access not only to our own inner voice, but also to the collective wisdom of the entire circle. This collective intelligence can access a "template" or pattern of action for the Core Group to discover its function within the larger social body. In a resonant field of love, the synergy of group energy magnetizes higher consciousness and wisdom for all. Each of us is often encouraged by the revelations or inspired insights coming forth from the group that can catalyze our own deeper knowing.

In its current most evolutionary form, the practice of "attuning to the design of creation" disrupts normal informational processing avenues and changes the nature of thinking itself.

Developing Criteria for Co-creative Decision Making

Before moving into the actual process of decision making, you may want to establish a set of criteria for making decisions that you feel aligned with as a team. You will be accessing inspired insights during this process.

Begin by selecting a facilitator and a scribe. (If you prefer, you could record the insights and play them back when the process is complete.)

The facilitator leads the group in an attunement and then poses the question: *"What is most important to each of us as criteria for decision making?"*

The scribe records the insights as they are spoken into the circle. When the process feels complete (after a long period of silence), the facilitator invites everyone to open their eyes and reconnect visually with others in the circle.

The scribe reads what has been revealed, and from these insights a key set of criteria for decision making is established for the group. (You might want to refer back to the "attuned alignment practices" that were offered for your discussion earlier in this chapter, to determine if there are additional criteria you want to add to your list.)

Process Guidelines

The process that follows is an extension of the Group Dialogue of Inspired Insights that you experienced earlier in Circle 4, Accessing Inner Wisdom. This practice is particularly useful when dealing with challenging issues and difficult decisions. Read through the following guidelines before moving into the experiential exercise.

- Select a facilitator and a member of the circle to take notes or record the session.
- Begin with a brief moment of silence to come into resonance and then read the criteria you have established and agreed upon for decision making.
- Ask each individual to check in and clear any emotional issues or hidden agendas that may stand in the way of clarity.
- Before beginning the process of inspired insights, frame your question. Speaking the issue or question with clarity will draw forth deeper insights.
- First get all the facts out on the table and discuss them with as much mental clarity as possible. Honor the rational mind and value the contribution it makes.
- Go within, relax, listen, and let go of any attachment to outcome. Release the thinking mind and prepare to receive guidance from the field.

- The facilitator might read the Guided Meditation for Co-creative Decision Making (directly below) to pose the question that the group has co-created.
- Each individual shares what she receives as it naturally arises. Often insights will come through a few members of the group as the others maintain resonance. It is important to speak only when inspired to do so. If everyone is attuned with one another, what is shared will ring true to each member of the circle. If insights come which seem conflicting, it is important to continue holding the resonant field, allowing the process to unfold organically.
- Beware of any tendency to over-ride an inner prompting or bodily feeling if there is a momentum building toward a particular solution. It can be challenging, but important for everyone's benefit, to say "this doesn't feel quite right to me."
- When it appears that all input has been shared, the facilitator gently brings the process to completion. Affirm areas of agreement and identify different perspectives as they arise. Synthesize what was shared.
- Take a moment to check in with your body and experience how the decision feels.
- If alignment has not occurred, re-attune and spend some quiet time alone. It is often beneficial to take a break, walk in nature, and be still.
- When everyone feels that clarity has been achieved, make appropriate choices that will move the decisions into action. *Remember that this is not a vote, but an attunement.*
- Always aim at coming into a deep level of alignment. Seek to arrive at a collective 'ah-ha' that everyone can stand solidly behind.
- Once a decision has been made, ask yourselves the following questions:
  - Do we have the human and financial resources to implement this decision?
  - Does this decision honor right timing?
  - Does this decision support the health, sustainability, and regeneration of all life?
  - Does this decision honor seven generations?
  - Does this decision embody the values we hold sacred?

Guided Meditation: Co-creative Decision Making

Once you have clarity regarding the issues that need to be addressed and the question you are facing, the facilitator slowly reads the following, remembering to pause between phrases.

Gently close your eyes and invite your body to relax . . . Take a few deep breaths and observe the activity of your mind and the flow of your feelings . . . There is no need to change your thoughts or feelings . . . just observe them.

(Pause)

We call forth those insights that will lead us to a decision that serves the highest good of all. . . We ask to be connected heart to heart. . . to have mental clarity and compassionate understanding . . . We ask that truth, love, and wisdom guide our way.

The facilitator then poses the question that the group has selected. Then she continues:

Now, tapping into your deeper knowing and this field of collective intelligence, speak as you feel moved to do so.

Members of the group speak at this time. When there is silence and it appears that everyone who feels called to do so has spoken, the facilitator says:

We give thanks for the insights we have received and the inspiration we experience . . . We acknowledge that all wisdom lies within and is available when we quiet our minds and surrender to loving presence.

(Pause)

Take another few deep breaths and gently move your hands and feet. When you're ready, open your eyes.

Return to the Guidelines given above to complete your decision-making process.

Moving from Inspiration into Action

SPEEDING UP

There may be occasions when a team faces what appears to be a critical point in time when action feels imperative. In this case, a number of Second-tier companies "forward the action" by suggesting that anyone on the team can make a decision—*so long as they seek advice from all affected parties and people with expertise in that particular arena.* They don't have to integrate and follow this advice, but they must seek it and genuinely take it into consideration before acting.

SLOWING DOWN

Often an inspiration that feels like clear guidance will emerge in a Co-creative Core. This may provoke a desire to "jump into action" and move full speed ahead on the guidance.

It is usually beneficial to re-evaluate priorities and review the inspiration by checking it out with the whole body. This refers to individually reflecting mentally on the decision and being aware of how it feels in your physical body. It also refers to tuning into the larger configuration of individuals who will be affected by the decision and determining if it is accurate for this "whole body."

Right timing may dictate that immediate action is not appropriate. Perhaps there needs to be a more solid foundation in place in order for the vision to successfully manifest. The inspiration might be reviewed as to the stages of development necessary. If an inspiration is held without attachment, the process of attunement will reveal right timing and right action.

Self-Governance

All life is intelligent, self-organizing and self-regulating:
from viruses and bacteria to plants, animals, and human beings.

STEPHEN HARROD BUHNER

LIVING FROM THE perspective of whole systems requires a shift from personality to presence, from First-tier to Second-tier thinking. True freedom in a co-creative society is possible when individuals operate from a sense of choice, personal responsibility, sovereignty, and unlimited possibility. While honoring commitments and agreements, each person is free to follow internal guidance rather than to respond from a sense of duty or obligation.

John Hagelin in *A Manual for a Perfect Government* speaks of the properties of nature's government and explains how the ideals of self-governance are based on the principles of natural law. In comparing nature to the highest order of self-governance, he suggests that both are:

- Maximally efficient
- Profoundly orderly (like snowflakes and atoms) and
- Inherently evolutionary and life supporting.

Self-governance emerges as the Self takes dominion in our lives and each of us takes full responsibility for our thoughts, feelings, and actions. It requires a high degree of maturity and a willingness to dive deeply into our authentic nature. As Self, we attune to the design of creation and allow life to live itself through us, effortlessly. We surrender to a benevolent wisdom and are guided to find our right relationships in perfect timing.

As we awaken to our true nature, we lay aside our local-self desires and cooperate with others to build integrated teams that are playing their part in birthing a new, more loving world.

Discuss

Share your thoughts about the emergence of self-governance in your personal life, within your Co-creative Core, and in society. Imagine a world in which everyone is taking full responsibility for his thoughts, feelings, and actions and is concerned with the well-being of all life. How can you and your team be models of self-governance in the world? Come into alignment as to how you want to apply the principles of self-governance as you pursue your shared destiny.

....my suggestion is not for more studies, not for more government grants,
not for trusting experts to solve the problems that face us.
It is for you to follow your own genius, for you to find in yourself
the still small spark of understanding that, with care, blossoms into
genuinely new solutions to what you yourself see as problems.

STEPHEN HARROD BUHNER

Out beyond ideas of wrongdoing and rightdoing,
there is a field. I'll meet you there.
When the soul lies down in that grass,
the world is too full to talk about.
Ideas, language, even the phrase "each other" doesn't make any sense.

RUMI - 13TH CENTURY

Deepening Practices

Following are exercises to be done on your own.

Journal

OBSERVE HOW SYNCHRONICITY shows up in your life. Make notes in your journal and share with your Core Group at the next meeting.

Practice going within to make decisions. Pay attention to how your body feels. Tune into the wisdom of your heart. Trust the Self and act on the guidance you receive. Keep track of how your process of making decisions evolves. Record in your journal any insights you receive.

Self-governance and Unconflicted Behavior

Joseph Chilton Pearce speaks of unconflicted behavior: a state in which our thoughts, words, emotions, and actions are in perfect alignment, "wherein heart and mind-brain resonate in synchronicity, opening us to levels of possibility beyond the ordinary." Unconflicted behavior is "the zone," the state of total inner-congruence and peace from which effortless manifestation always arises.

John Amaral offers these 5 keys to creating unconflicted behavior:

1. Decide what you want
2. Eliminate doubt
3. Stay in action
4. Remain flexible
5. Stay grateful

Be mindful of this principle and observe how on track you are in being unconflicted within yourself. This can become very subtle as you observe your thoughts, feelings, and actions over time. Be compassionate and non-judgmental as you move into greater coherence and self-governance.

CIRCLE 9

Birthing a New World

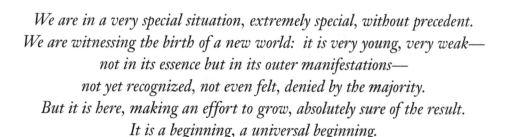

We are in a very special situation, extremely special, without precedent.
We are witnessing the birth of a new world: it is very young, very weak—
not in its essence but in its outer manifestations—
not yet recognized, not even felt, denied by the majority.
But it is here, making an effort to grow, absolutely sure of the result.
It is a beginning, a universal beginning.
So, it is an absolutely unexpected and unpredictable adventure.

THE MOTHER, MIRRA ALFANSO, SPOKEN IN THE 1960's

Inner alignment with the present moment opens your consciousness
and brings it into alignment with the whole.
The whole, the totality of life, then acts through you.

ECKHART TOLLE

We have begun to awaken to the fact that our living planet is the source of
all real wealth and the foundation of our own existence.
We must now look to living systems as our teacher,
for our survival depends on discovering new ways of living—
and making our living—that embody life's wisdom.

DAVID C. KORTEN

As living cells in the planetary body,
we are being called to express our unique magnificence
through meaningful and chosen work in service to the greater whole.
Once we have discovered our soul's purpose and aligned with our team
around a shared destiny, we want to express our full potential
and play our part in transforming society.   In our own way,
we become social architects contributing to the birth of a new world.

All over the world Core Groups are naturally converging with one another,
connecting co-creators in every sector of society, exploring new forms
which reflect whole-systems understanding.

It is this convergence that creates the synergy to more fully actualize
the individuals involved, allowing each of us to tap the power and
resources of the collective. It is this interaction of innovative elements
that shifts consciousness and jumps the entire system to a new order.

The essence of co-creation—working from the inside out, combining the
spiritual practices of resonance, love, and inner wisdom
with outer actions in the world—manifests as collective positive change.

Our "giving back" may express itself in a variety of forms—be it an
entrepreneurial venture, a nonprofit organization, a spiritually-motivated
social activity, or an environmental or political project.
All expressions contain the seed of a new social form which
combines the principles of co-creation with new forms of leadership
and the self-organizing laws inherent in nature.

Our greatest pleasure is to fully express our love and unique genius by sharing our gifts with others. We create from a consciousness of wholeness. Our reward is the freedom to be authentic, working cooperatively with those we love and respect. The distinction between work and play dissolves as all actions are expressions of the Impulse of Creation, offered as a service and blessing. Our love manifests as the transformation of society and the birth of a new, more loving world.

Birthing a New World

A system in balance and functioning well is difficult to change,
but as a system falls into disorder, change becomes more and more feasible
and finally inevitable. At that inevitable point, the least bit of
coherence can bring to order the whole disorderly array.
Which direction the change takes depends on the nature
of the chaotic attractor that lifts the chaos into its new order.
If that chaotic attractor is demonic, the old cycle simply repeats itself,
which seems to have been historically the case for our species.
But if the chaotic attractor were benevolent or "Divine,"
the new order would have to be of that same nature.

JOSEPH CHILTON PEARCE

Core Groups are formative units of the emerging culture.
Even now, networks of human-scale communities composed of such
small resonant groups are forming the basis for the cultural reformation of the world.

BARBARA MARX HUBBARD

WE ARE LIVING at a moment of tremendous global change—a time when the whole social system is shifting. A century ago, one's world was one's town. Today globalization and technological innovations have expanded our sense of the world and have touched and affected all of our lives. In this age of communication, there are officially more mobile devices than people in the world, and they're multiplying five times faster than we are. (There are more cell phones worldwide than toilets, toothbrushes, or refrigerators!) Ordinary citizens have greater connectivity today than the President of the U.S. had during the 1990's! And as more of us have access to the internet, there is an explosion of creativity, connectivity, and opportunity occurring globally.

Many of us find ourselves in the precarious situation of walking in two worlds, trying to navigate in the existing social structures while simultaneously creating a new culture. As we bring our dreams into full expression in the world, we are required to use our gift of discernment. How do we keep our hearts open in the face of social injustice, intolerance, and economic inequality? How can our contribution to the betterment of society be meaningful and effective? How can we develop our leadership skills to reflect this new consciousness? How do we remain true to our values and align our *doing* with our *being*, moment by moment?

Each of us has our own unique calling in response to this great wave of change. As both our internal and external worlds are shifting, it is necessary to turn our attention to focus on what is creative and possible rather than trying to fix that which is basically dysfunctional and decaying. This shift calls for nothing less than a fundamental change of consciousness, requiring an in-depth review of our worldview, principles, and values.

The transformation of our current institutions—government, education, healthcare, energy management, business, etc.—is critical to ensuring the quality of life for future generations. It is an evolutionary imperative that we learn to cooperate with one another and follow Gandhi's directive by "being the change we want for the world."

Drawing upon the inherent wisdom of nature, we join our Co-creative Core with other Core Groups, aligning our gifts with one another to co-create projects, organizations, and institutions that are living organisms: dynamic, whole, flexible, and connected. Through this mutual support, we are able to tap into the power and resources of the greater whole. We experience that self-organizing systems enhance both the creativity and the effectiveness of all who are involved.

Aligning heart to heart with one another, we cluster as community, drawing inspiration from one another—as we call on the expertise and intelligence of the collective. Joining with others in spiritually-motivated social action, we foster the emergence of a caring society in which each of us feels empowered and liberated to be all that we can be—giving our gifts, expressing our love, and serving our families, communities, and planet.

As we evolve personally and stabilize as true co-creators, we move from an experience of community to one of deep communion with others. We become the "new person," a Whole Being who is living the "new story" of love, trust, empowerment, and connection. We unite with others to birth the "new society" that humanity has been dreaming into reality for eons.

Guided Meditation and Inspired Insights Process: Envisioning a New World

The facilitator slowly reads this meditation aloud, remembering to pause between phrases. In this exercise, you will be calling on inspired insights to envision together a just, sustainable, and loving world. You may want to play soft music in the background. Allow 10-15 minutes for the sharing of images that arise as you access your collective wisdom and paint the picture of an imagined future world that embodies the values you hold sacred. One person's speaking tends to inspire another's and activates a co-creative intelligence.

Gently close your eyes and take a few deep breaths. . . Feel your body relaxing as you let go of plans for the future and memories of the past. Rest in the present moment.

(Pause)

Breathing slowly and deeply . . . feel the energy of life moving through every cell of your body. . . bringing a sense of aliveness, deep peace, and well-being.

(Pause)

In your mind's eye, begin to imagine a new world unfolding before you. . . a world of justice, beauty, and fulfillment for all. . . a co-creative culture. . . an empathic society. Take a moment to look around . . . See and feel the beauty of this new world.

(Pause)

Now, place yourself in this environment. Feel your being coming into perfect resonance with all your surroundings . . . radiant, vibrant, centered, whole.

(Pause)

Now, see yourself fulfilling your soul's purpose . . . expressing your mastery . . . sharing your gifts and talents . . . Notice what are you doing . . . Notice how this feels in your body.

(Pause for 1 minute)

Sense yourself joining with your perfect partners . . . those who share your destiny . . . your ideal team-mates . . . Notice that your team is perfectly balanced, resonant, and complete. . . All the gifts and resources that are needed for the fulfillment of your mission are available. . . . Notice how you feel.

(Pause for 1 minute)

In this new world, every field of endeavor has shifted to a higher frequency . . . All of humanity is empowered and supported . . . every true need is being filled . . . There is plenty for everyone . . . Creativity abounds. . . The division between work and play is gone.

(Pause)

What do you know about this new co-creative culture—this compassionate society? Paint the picture of the world that you dream of creating. Share images and inspirations that arise out of the collective wisdom in this resonant field.

(Allow at least 5 - 10 minutes for many responses to come forth. When it feels complete and there is a significant pause in the sharing, continue with the guided meditation.)

Take another deep breath, relaxing into this feeling of satisfaction and deep peace. . . Know that as you envision, you are bringing this new culture into reality . . . Feel the radiance of your heart overflowing, sending love to all life . . . to every village and city . . . to every member of our human family . . . Affirm that what you have seen, felt, and declared is happening now! Feel loving presence moving through you and this group, rekindling hope, faith, and trust in all of humanity.

(Pause)

Now, with another deep breath, become aware of yourself seated in this room and, when you're ready, open your eyes, and connect with each person in the circle in silence.

Take a few notes in your journals and then share your insights in the larger circle.

Check-In

As you check-in, speak about any shifts that have occurred within you since you first began meeting and working with the material in this *Handbook*. Which co-creative practices are the most relevant in your life today? How are these changes reflected in your home, your work, your relationships, and elsewhere in your world? What are the most important lessons you've learned about yourself?

Living Between Worlds

*There is overwhelming evidence that human consciousness is evolving,
moving from collective tribal living, where the individual was totally embedded
in the life patterns of the collective; through a gradual, often painful,
process of individuation, with the emphasis on the will and sovereignty
of the individual; to what is emerging in our time: a conscious return
to collectivism where individuated, or self-actualized,
individuals voluntarily—sometimes temporarily—
pool their consciousness in a search for the elusive collective intelligence
that can help us to overcome the stupendous challenges now facing us
as a species as a consequence of how our developmental trajectory
has manifested on the physical plane thus far.*

RIA BAECK AND HELEN TITCHEN BEETH

We recognize that we are in a transitional phase, an era when outer forms and structures often do not reflect our inner knowing. The institutions and systems that we interact with on a daily basis may not support the values and ideals we cherish. This paradox requires a skillful navigation between worlds; we are being asked to become "spiral wizards." It becomes necessary to simultaneously deal with the increasing demands of our modern society while opening to radically new ways of being. We are learning to honor the gifts of each stage of our personal and collective evolution, as we acknowledge the whole-systems transformation that is occurring at this time.

A new world is seeking to be born through us—one that reflects a synthesis of the wisdom of the past and the unlimited possibilities of the future. It is invisibly growing while, simultaneously, the world we have known is breaking down. Concurrently, we are creating and letting go—building and dissolving. We are called to compassionate understanding for our personal journey and for the lives of others as we find our perfect place in the whole. We are learning that we don't have to wait until a system breaks down before making the changes that are needed to nurture and enhance life. Each of us, in our own way, can "gentle the birth" of the new culture.

As we awaken to our full potential as co-creators, there is a reconfiguration of our individual behavior. Some of us are drawn to bring our gifts and awareness to the mainstream—to evolve practices and systems that feel stagnant and stifling to human creativity. Others of us are bridge builders, focusing on creating connections between the old paradigm and the emerging future. Still others are encoded with the patterns of the new world and are pioneering innovative processes and social structures. Addressing the needs at all levels of transformation is vital as we compassionately hospice the old and joyfully midwife the new.

Discuss

Discuss any challenges you may be experiencing as you release the old and embrace the new.

- Do you feel that you are living between worlds? If so, what is that like for you?
- What is most challenging for you as you navigate these changes?
- What do you need from your Core Group to support you in this transitional time?
- What do you feel is the greatest gift you have to offer to assist others as they navigate the challenges of today?

When you are complete, capture any insights in your journals.

The Convergence of Cores

---◆---

EVERY GROUP HAS natural, multiple connections. As part of a living system, each Core will begin to seek out, by attraction, other Cores that are complementary to its function. Often this link-up occurs through a connecting point, such as shared purpose, or through a connector who holds membership in several groups at once. Regardless of how this occurs, Cores must carefully blend during the early, delicate stages of convergence so as to not become disempowered, overshadowed, or dysfunctional by this merging. Right timing and right relationship must be honored for this synthesis to hold and evolve.

Just as cells in a fetus join to build specific organs—heart cells clustering with heart cells, kidney cells with kidney cells, brain cells with brain cells—it is natural for Co-creative Cores to seek out and join with other teams to gain support in fulfilling their purpose. Like cells in our bodies, each team or organization is performing a unique and vital function within the body of humanity.

Core groups join with one another through an organic self-organizing process. As each group finds and attracts other teams or organizations performing similar functions, alliances begin to form. Artists, educators, scientists, and others in every sector of society coalesce to build the organism of the emerging culture. And in this process, as the whole is formed by its parts, *it is the whole which is informing the parts* so they know how and what to build. Eventually, a balance will occur where all converging Cores find their right place in the pattern.

As each group learns to be entrepreneurial and self-sufficient, there is a natural tendency to share resources with others for mutual support and empowerment. This clustering and alignment of co-creative teams is occurring spontaneously around the world as we self-organize into new configurations and transition from a self-centered competitive society into one that is more cooperative, caring, and mutually beneficial. *The following are just two examples of how your team might support this natural process of convergence of Cores in your local community.*

Guide the Organic Process of Convergence

You might begin the process of convergence by networking locally to bring representative members of existing teams or businesses together around shared purpose. You can also use the power of the internet to locate those groups and individuals who appear to be in alignment with your mission and values. A number of new companies, social networks, and apps are available to facilitate this process. *Remember that only teams that have stabilized and aligned around shared values, vision, and mission will be able to successfully converge with other teams.*

The following are basic steps you might take to bring groups together in your area:

- Determine who the natural networkers are in your community and solicit their assistance in locating the groups and organizations that feel resonant with your values.
- Invite these groups to come together to learn how you might serve one another.
- Invite each individual or team to share their vision, purpose, and function as part of a whole system.
- Model basic co-creative practices to bring harmony and efficiency to this process of joining group genius: create and maintain group resonance; use the Council Process; practice inner listening, etc.
- Look for points of convergence such as complementary vocations and functions. Cluster members around these points.
- Eventually, you will want to match needs and resources with one another by expressing what you need to fulfill your team's mission and sharing what you have to offer other Cores.
- Don't rush the process. This may take weeks or even months. Enjoy meeting new people, surrender to what wants to happen, and don't try to force or control the outcome.
- Create structural forms for ongoing communication and use the process of inspired insights to make decisions and guide your actions.
- Hold the intent to manifest results that are mutually beneficial and fulfilling for each Co-creative Core or organization.

Create a Peace Room and Office of the Future in Your Community

In 1984 Barbara Marx Hubbard ran for Vice President of the U.S. proposing the creation of a new social function called the Peace Room or Office for the Future.

The Peace Room is focused not only on peace but also on the synergistic coordination of everything that is working toward a viable, sustainable, evolving world. The name "Peace Room" is used to compare the sophistication that is involved in running the "War Room" in the U.S. Department of Defense. The purpose of this new social function is to enable the convergence of social innovations at the highest level of power.

In a War Room, the military tracks enemies and strategizes how to defeat them. In a Peace Room, social pioneers identify, map, connect, and communicate the successes, breakthroughs, and models that work. Peace, in this context, means peace through co-creation, through the full expression of human creativity in cooperation with nature, with one another, and with the deeper design of evolution.

The Peace Room, as a social synergy process, integrates the Office of the Future to harness the collective intelligence, wisdom, and consciousness of a community to facilitate the repatterning of society to a higher order of consciousness, freedom, and synergy.

The Office has four functions:

- To scan for breakthroughs in all sectors of society—including health, government, science, education, media, business, and the arts
- To map these innovations according to function and geography to discover the pattern and design of what works
- To connect people and projects for greater cooperation and effectiveness (the convergence of Cores)
- To communicate via all media the stories of our human family's successes and model projects

This process can work at the local, national, or global level. For example, Ambassadors to the U.N. are being asked to establish Peace Rooms to discover what works in their countries.

You might create a Peace Room and Office of the Future in your community to support the convergence of Cores.

The Wheel of Co-Creation

The following diagram depicts Barbara Hubbard's Wheel of Co-Creation, a holistic structure representing 12 sectors or vital functions of any community. The Wheel is designed to help communities develop a whole system model of evolutionary change by bringing together Co-creative Cores in the Peace Room Process.

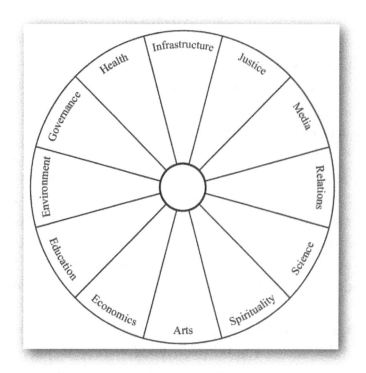

For additional information about The Peace Room, Office of the Future, and the Wheel of Co- Creation, go to www.evolve.org.

Cooperative Entrepreneurship

⸺ ❦ ⸺

*The quality of results produced by any system depends on the
quality of awareness from which people in the system operate.
The formula for a successful change process is not "form follows function,"
but "form follows consciousness." The structure of awareness
and attention determines the pathway along which a situation unfolds.*

OTTO SHARMER

COOPERATIVE ENTREPRENEURSHIP IS a relatively new business model that provides a powerful initiative for re-integrating human culture into its natural environment by always considering the effect of human effort on the larger community. It releases creativity and provides a vehicle for the fulfillment of our soul's purpose and shared destiny.

In his seminal book, *Reinventing Organizations*, Frederic Laloux suggests that as we become more aware and move from First-tier to Second-tier consciousness, our trust increases and our need to control decreases. We do our best and learn from our mistakes, accepting that every experience is an opportunity to evolve and grow. We shift from external to internal yardsticks—from a focus on organization to a focus on mission. We value humility and acknowledge that we are a node in the whole, rather than the hub or center of any particular project.

The world of business and nonprofit organizations is being transformed through the practical application of win/win practices and the expanded awareness that humanity is bringing to this arena. We can no longer, nor do we want to, rely on government or large bureaucracies to support our creativity. In a conscious business, co-creators express themselves fully, responsibly, creatively, and joyfully—and make valuable contributions to the greater community. We learn to become self-supporting and self-generating. The organization becomes a living organism—shifting and transforming to meet the needs of a rapidly changing world. People find their perfect place based on right relationship, going where they are invited and trusting their inner guidance.

To manifest successfully, basic principles of good business are needed: integrity, service, perseverance, excellence, commitment, vision, strategy, communication, accountability, efficiency, and more. Some Co-creative Cores shift from focusing on a particular project to creating an entrepreneurial enterprise, so that they can support themselves financially. Risk is minimized when individuals can look beyond their personal talents and call upon the creativity of a resonant group. If the team is balanced and all essential functions are represented, the possibility of achieving financial success and personal fulfillment is optimized.[5]

In cooperative entrepreneurship, the dichotomy between work and play ends. Gone are the barriers between inner and outer work and between spiritual and secular life. Cooperative entrepreneurship transforms the workplace from an arena of effort and struggle to an oasis of cooperation and creativity.

As a Core Group begins to practice this new social form it is appropriate to choose, affirm, and declare the success of your work as a model of the change you would like to see in the world.

Characteristics of cooperative entrepreneurship include:

- Honoring and empowering all stakeholders
- Providing a quality product or service of true value
- Tapping group creativity and collective intelligence
- Applying good business skills
- Responsibly rewarding everyone
- Focusing on multiple bottom lines (people, planet, profit, future generations, etc.)
- Being self-regenerating and sustainable
- Being stimulating and self rewarding
- Enhancing relationships
- Focusing on public, as well as private benefit

---

5 Remember, a balanced co-creative team includes at least one visionary, a resonance holder, a systems builder, and an implementer. Together, they provide the spiritual, emotional, mental, and physical balance that creates a whole system or holon.

Discuss

Discuss the characteristics of cooperative entrepreneurship. Modify or add to the list above, to reflect your own understanding and experience. What do you feel is important for the success of a business or project that embodies the principles of co-creation and is reflective of the emerging paradigm? Use your list as criteria to guide your group's venture and assist you in your decision-making process.

If you are willing, share your ideas about cooperative entrepreneurship on our website, so that others can benefit from your experience: www.cocreatorshandbook.com.

New Forms of Leadership

Empowered Leadership

NEW STRUCTURES AND processes require a new kind of leader: a person who is self-responsible, aware of her gifts and capabilities, and is willing to assume authority as appropriate. Empowered leaders guide the team when they know best, and they respect everyone on their team as equals and as valued members. They foster the awareness that each member of the team is equally unique and vital to the whole. They have a gift for focalizing, facilitating, and bringing the best out of everyone, and they know when to step back and empower other members to guide the team. *In the co-creative model, we are all simultaneously leading and following, and we have the humility to know when to step forward and when to step back.*

Empowered leaders co-create and maintain the vision and spirit of the team and assure that both collective and individual mastery are valued. Through her dedication and commitment to the mission, the new leader calls forth the best in others and inspires them to go for excellence. While traditional managers are expected to "do things right," the evolved leader "does the right thing." She earns the Core's trust by being consistent and accountable and by making intentions evident. Mistakes are forgiven, even encouraged. Failures of the past are re-contextualized as "learning experiences."

Author and trainer Jack Canfield suggests that leaders can create high performance teams and empower others as leaders by:

- Knowing their own strengths and weaknesses and demonstrating humility and authenticity
- Holding themselves and all members of the team accountable
- Inspiring their team with a clear, compelling vision
- Listening for what is possible and learning from others
- Coaching others to take on leadership roles—through deep listening and skillful questioning

- Practicing gratitude and acknowledging others to build trust, enthusiasm, and commitment in those around them

Process: New Leadership

Take a few minutes to attune with one another before the facilitator offers the following questions to invite inspired insights. Remember to pause after each question to allow each person to access their response. When you are complete with this process, you might capture your insights in your journals.

What qualities do you feel are most important in today's leaders?

Who do you know in your private life or in the public arena who is modeling empowered leadership?

When and how do you exhibit your leadership abilities?

Evolutionary Co-leadership, Holacracy, and Chaordic Organizations

> *The point is not to make everyone equal; it is to allow all employees to grow into the strongest, healthiest version of themselves.*
>
> FREDERIC LALOUX

Business consultant Alain Gauthier suggests that co-leadership, which combines the best of individual gifts and creativity with true synergy and collective wisdom, is most appropriate for leading-edge organizations. In this model, leadership is shared, distributed, or collective. Leadership is considered to be a relational process, rather than a position, and is based on open dialogue and mutuality. It cuts across boundaries and is simultaneously top-down, bottom-up, and circular to generate innovation and address complex challenges. "Co-leadership challenges the traditional distinction between leaders and followers" to generate a new culture that calls forth the genius of the individuals and the team.

Holacracy is a social technology that "separates role from soul," disconnecting the fusion of identity that people sometimes hold with their job titles. In this mode of operation, people don't have a job; instead, they fill a number of roles. Meetings follow a process to ensure that all voices are heard and that no one can dominate decision-making. The organization adapts and corrects constantly, based on the problems and opportunities that people sense. The intent in this model is to ensure that no valid objection is overlooked and that collective intelligence is honored.

New institutions and entities are being birthed daily around the globe, blending the characteristics of chaos and order—what Dee Hock, the founder of VISA, calls a chaordic organization. Self-regulating, self-governing, flexible, and able to adapt to change swiftly—these organizations are contributing to the birth of a new economic and social paradigm. By aligning groups around shared purpose and ethical principles, chaordic entities are able to create and govern diversity and complexity that a centralized system or bureaucratic structure cannot readily manage. They follow the pattern of nature, which may appear to be disorderly and messy, but is ultimately coherent when viewed from an expanded perspective.

Discuss

What other models of leadership are you aware of that are emerging at this time? What evidence do you see that institutions are shifting to a partnership model? Are you aware of any businesses or organizations that are experimenting with co-leadership, holocracy, or a chaordic process? (If you are willing, please go to www.cocreatorshandbook.com and post your ideas there so that others can benefit from your expertise.)

As models of leadership shift from organizational hierarchies
with leaders at the top to more distributed, shared networks,
a lot changes. For those networks to work with real awareness,
many people will need to be deeply committed to cultivating their capacity

*to serve what's seeking to emerge. That's why I think that
'becoming a real human being,' really is the primary leadership issue of our time,
but on a scale never required before. It's a very old idea
that may actually hold the key to a new age of global democracy.*

BETTY SUE FLOWERS

The Sharing Caring Economy

THE SHARING ECONOMY is a rapidly-growing ecosystem made possible by the advent of the smart phone. It is built around the sharing of human, physical, and intellectual resources and includes the shared creation, production, distribution, trade, and consumption of goods and services by different people and organizations. This economy promotes a "we-based" culture where the wider community and the greater good are considered. Health, happiness, trust, and sustainability are notable characteristics. Sharing is seen as a positive attribute; and people who share are celebrated, encouraged, and supported.

This emerging economy is characterized by different forms of value exchange and is a hybrid encompassing the following aspects: swapping, exchanging, open source, collective purchasing, collaborative consumption, shared ownership, democratization of online higher education, co-operatives, alternative and local currencies, recycling and upcycling, trading used goods, person-to-person borrowing and lending, pay-as-you-use systems, microfinancing, social media, crowdfunding, and crowdsourcing. Idle resources are reallocated or traded with those who want or need them to create an efficient, equitable, closed loop, or circular system. Goods and services are designed for sustainability rather than obsolescence; and rules, policies, laws, and standards are created via a democratic system that enables and encourages mass participation at all levels. Technology and social networks are vital elements that enable the flow of communications and support the sharing of information.

While the Sharing Economy is currently in its infancy, in 2016 there are over 8000 companies worldwide offering shared experiences in the arenas of: places to stay, transport, finance, food and drink, pets, and more. It is a new and alternative socio-economic system which embeds sharing and collaboration at its heart, across all aspects of social and economic life. The people who are driving this new economy are sometimes called Generation Share.

The Caring Economy shifts society's focus away from money first to care first and operates in tandem with the Sharing Economy. Those who participate in this economy remember that the Earth and every part of the material world is a gift and that we are here to share with one another.

As temporary stewards of the money that moves through our lives, we support a circular flow based on sharing, caring, loving, giving, and receiving. Remembering that we are all one global family, we trust that there is enough for everyone and that we can take care of each other. We give our power to Spirit, rather than to money.

In the corporate world—job sharing, on-site childcare, flextime, telecommuting, working at home, and sabbaticals are current examples of the caring economy. As more of us acknowledge that the world is a global village and put care first, we are building a strong economic foundation for ourselves and for future generations to come.

Discuss

Are you participating in the sharing economy? What trends do you see emerging along these lines in your community? Do you feel a shift occurring at the national and global levels? Discuss these operating principles of the new caring economy and make any additions that feel appropriate. Share your ideas here, so that others can benefit: www.cocreatorshandbook.com.

- Put care first! Care about "all your relations." Put people and life first!
- Empower all those connected with you and, where appropriate, organize around the people you serve, rather than around a product.
- Remember that money flows in a nonlinear way. There are times when giving precedes receiving—and vice versa.
- Champion and support the elderly, women, and children—who are often sources of inspiration in the caring economy.
- Focus on niches and communities of interest, delivering unique products and services.
- Let your information flow; share your knowledge with others.
- Keep your communications as simple as possible.
- Protect and build your good name. Trust is not easy to establish, and those who gain their customer's trust will reap the long-term rewards.
- Focus on the value you deliver, not just the costs you save or profits you make.

- Have a long-term vision of where you want to go. Remember that we are citizens of an increasingly connected planet. For the long-term stability and prosperity of our world, we cannot continue to ignore the injustice, poverty, and famine that so many of our fellow citizens must daily endure.
- Embrace change and flow with life.

New Ways of Living

Life from its beginning more than three billion years ago did not take over the planet by combat, but by network, by cooperation, by partnership.

FRITJOF CAPRA

*As the new emerges, some people will feel called upon to form groups that reflect the enlightened consciousness.... Enlightened collectives will fulfill an important function in the arising of the new consciousness.....
and can be a vortex for awareness that will accelerate the planetary shift.*

ECKHART TOLLE

As WE MOVE toward the next stage of human evolution, large numbers of conscious, resonant teams working with other small teams are creating sustainable communities that model the new society we dream is possible. These communities design their businesses, culture, and programs to align with nature's ability to thrive. They think in terms of whole systems: process, pattern, context, and relationships. Their focus is on the well being of the whole, in addition to the well-being of the individual. Cohousing, intentional communities, eco-villages and social networks are providing new structures that facilitate connection, enhance cooperation, offer mutual benefit, and build co-creative community for many members of our human family.

These new communities encourage diversity and authenticity. They are places to share common ideas, beliefs, values, and traditions. Although there are many new forms, they have the following in common: they feel like home, and they provide a sense of safety in which members can be held and can grow, learn, deepen, and evolve.

Intentional Communities

*Small islands of coherence in a sea of chaos
have the capacity to shift the entire system to a higher order.*

ILYA PRIGOGENE, NOBEL LAUREATE

The next Buddha may not be an individual, but an enlightened community.

THICH NHAT HANH

What calls individuals to live in communities which they intentionally create as an expression of their values and ideals? What are the common elements motivating a shift in lifestyle that most often requires a departure from the mainstream culture? Is the growing movement of intentional communities a passing trend or an indication of the wave of the future?

As humanity takes an evolutionary leap from one paradigm to another, social pioneers are modeling new possibilities in every realm of human endeavor. Some individuals may be drawn to community life for social, political, ecological, personal, or spiritual reasons. Communities that blossom and endure are comprised of members who are magnetized together by resonance and a unified purpose. They desire to be living and working in a co-creative environment that allows for the full expression of their soul qualities. Often they view their community as an island of hope and coherence in a chaotic and confused world.

Emerging at an ever-increasing rate, intentional communities are a natural reflection of the evolution of consciousness. They allow for the modeling of a holistic integrated lifestyle, where the influences of the external culture are minimized. In addition, they can serve as "cocooning centers" for personal and collective metamorphosis. Individuals are held in a safety net of love and acceptance in the midst of inner reconfiguration. The natural yearning to belong is fulfilled as each person remembers his interconnectedness with all life.

Intentional communities also provide a more conscious, caring environment for young people whose destiny may be to usher in this new co-creative culture and manifest innovative solutions to the massive problems that confront us. Much of the distress of young people these days is that their brilliance is not seen or supported. They often do not have outlets for their creativity and are blocked in their expression. During this transitional phase communities are vital to providing a highly nurturing living context for these wise young beings.[6]

Discuss

- Does your current living situation meet your needs for community?
- Has your lifestyle changed fundamentally in the recent past?
- Do new ways of living appeal to you?
- What benefit might there be for you to explore a new way of living?
- In what ways are you transitioning into a co-creative lifestyle?

Completion Ceremony

To honor the deep internal and external changes that may have occurred for members of your group, co-create a ceremony that reflects the individuality of each member of the Core and the shared values of the whole. You may want to do this in nature.

Co-create an altar with candles, flowers, and the gifts of the Earth. Be sure that each member of your team places an object that symbolizes his unique purpose and creative expression on the altar.

Devise a meaningful ritual that allows each of you to share what you have learned and where you see yourself in six months, one year, and in five years. Express your gratitude

---

6 Hummingbird Community, nestled in the Sangre de Cristo Mountains of northern New Mexico, was founded in 1996 by the co-authors and four other members of Global Family. As social pioneers, the members of this spiritually-based eco-village are dedicated to living the principles of co-creation, releasing old belief systems that are rooted in conditioning, and opening to the freshness of what naturally wants to emerge that is rooted in love. Hummingbird aspires to be a place where diversity is valued and where people live in partnership with one another and with nature, in a spirit of reverence, cooperation, integrity, trust, and compassion. (www.hummingbirdcommunity.org.)

for all lessons, large and small, and for your heartfelt connection to the members of your group.

Close with the Silent Greeting

As your group nears the completion of this phase of its work together, use the Silent Greeting to share your love and respect for one another. If necessary, refer to Circle 2 for specific instructions. Be sure to play heartful music in the background and *speak only with your hearts and eyes.* Drink in the magnificence of each person in your Core Group—the One expressing as many.

Celebrate!

Either at the end of this session or in the near future, plan a party to celebrate one another. Each person could bring his favorite dish of food and a musical instrument. You may want to include special friends and family members as you commemorate the completion of one phase of your collective journey and the beginning of another!

May you be richly blessed and fully empowered
to play your part in birthing a new, more loving world!

Deepening Practices

Following are exercises to be done on your own.

Be a Mindful Consumer and Investor

Pay attention to the choices you and your family are making as consumers.

- Are your consumption patterns in alignment with your values?
- Do you buy from independently-owned local businesses?
- When you make a purchase, ask yourself: Is this fulfilling a need or a desire? Will this item enhance my life or deplete my energy? Tune into your body's intelligence to sense what feels right.
- Do you consider the impact your purchases have on other people and the Earth?
- Are you conscious of where you invest your personal resources?
- Do you bank locally?
- Do you contribute to groups that are congruent with your values?

Co-create a Positive Future

Visualize the success of your project or venture and the fulfillment of each member's life purpose. Share your vision for the future with a kindred spirit or describe this in your journal. As you envision and deeply feel into your dream, you begin to bring it into reality.

New structures, institutions, agreements, and ways of doing things are springing up like green shoots through the rubble of our dysfunctional civilization. I don't think there has ever been a time in human history when so many new ways of doing things have appeared in so short a time. They reveal an amazing degree of ingenuity, an awesome readiness to experiment and create. Even though these emergent and often embryonic systems sometimes look fringe or marginal, they are the seeds of the future.

JOANNA MACY

Awakening in Our Dream

Those who tell the stories rule society.

PLATO

The world as we know it is built on a story.
To be a change agent is first to disrupt the existing Story of the World,
and second to tell a new Story of the World,
so that those entering the space between stories have a place to go.

CHARLES EISENSTEIN

Because of the interconnectedness of all minds, affirming a positive vision
may be about the most sophisticated action any one of us can take.

WILLIS HARMAN

IN THE MIDST of these challenging and complex times there is a great opportunity to create a message of hope, a new cultural narrative, a vision of possibility. This new story is a vision grounded in our intelligence, awareness, and capacity to know who we truly are.

As Thomas Berry so beautifully expressed, we are between stories and our hearts yearn for a new story—one that we know to be true because it resonates so deeply in our hearts. Many of us are devoting our lives to bringing this story into reality. There is a call from the future—from generations yet to be born or perhaps from our own future Self. What is the legacy that we wish to leave behind? What is the story that we want to live into?

The creation of a new story invokes bold imagination, invites new language, and requires a break from habit and from the familiar. Let's go within and imagine the world that we dream is possible. Let us dream together to co-create the loving world that we hold in our hearts.

Imagine. . .

An emanation of radiant golden sunlight is appearing on the horizon, as we gaze out onto the world. The birds alert us with their joyful song to the birth of a new dawn. All life is awakening to a worldly reality that was once held only in the realm of dreams.

Imagine. . .

The air is light and fresh. It is the springtime of our evolutionary journey. We have moved beyond a cultural dark night of the soul and have awakened as our Selves.

Imagine. . .

We are awakening in our dream.

There is a generosity of spirit, a natural desire to share and to care for one another—across borders, racial differences, and ethnic classes. Diversity is honored and is cultivated as essential. We have come to understand that it is through a rich expression of diversity that nature, and thus humanity, survives and thrives. Each person's uniqueness is appreciated and celebrated. We listen deeply with curiosity and openness in order to honor each other's points of view. High telepathy, synchronicity, and compassionate action guide us as we co-create this new world.

Loving, supportive families have once again become the nucleus of society. Interpersonal growth and the nurturing of soul qualities have become the primary focus of intimate relationships. Our communities are thriving as places of safety and well being.

The breakdown of social, political, and religious institutions worldwide has become compost for the birth of a global community based on mutual respect, cooperation, and love. Society's challenges are recognized as inter-related and inter-dependent. Issues related to poverty, racism, crime, corruption, and environmental devastation are understood to emerge from the same root: the illusion that we are separate from each other, nature, and the Source of our being.

In this new story, we are aware that we are deeply interconnected. We come together in heartfelt resonance to co-create solutions. Successful models and best practices are freely shared and wisely replicated through open-source technologies. Social movements, innovations, and breakthroughs are communicated instantaneously via the internet, allowing for rapid transformation in every aspect of life.

Throughout the world, rich and poor, young and old are working side by side—building homes, planting gardens, restoring the fabric of our eco-system and re-building healthy communities in both urban and rural settings. An understanding of integrated systems is being demonstrated through the application of permaculture, bio-dynamic farming, regenerative design, renewable energy systems, appropriate technology, and green building practices. Having respect for the ecological web, people are living simple, regenerative, and balanced lifestyles. Our relationship with the life-supporting systems of our bio-regional watersheds has transformed our cultures. Water is treasured as a sacred resource. We have become very aware of both the resiliency and fragility of our precious planet.

Scientists who are making great advances in technology—biotech, nanotech, artificial intelligence, and other arenas—are aware of their power to create or destroy, and they take responsibility to foster and protect the evolution of our species.

Knowing that babies are greatly influenced by the manner in which they are nurtured within the womb and brought forth into the world, couples prepare for childbirth before conception, consciously calling forth the Spirit of the child. At the time of birth, the elders tune into the "song of the soul" and lovingly offer it as a guiding light for the child's journey through life. When it is time to complete the earthly journey, the physical form is released at will. There is no fear of death, as there is an inherent understanding of the eternal nature of life in all dimensions.

Schools have turned their attention to serve their communities, engaging young people in the restoration of the ecological and social fabric. The leaders of these new institutions know that the task of education is to nurture the development of creative, imaginative individuals who can navigate through an era of tremendous change.

Children have learned to listen deeply to all aspects of their being—body, mind, and Spirit— and to speak from their hearts. Growing up in environments that cultivate a field of safety, trust, and compassion, they learn to love and respect themselves and to honor their intuition as well as their intellect. They feel their connection to the stars, while being firmly rooted to Earth. As members of an evolving species, they know that they are consciousness itself having a worldly experience!

Evolutionary eco-villages have emerged worldwide as resource and educational centers for nearby cities and towns. As living laboratories for the new culture, land-based intentional communities are hubs of cross pollination between traditions, generations, economic classes, and urban and rural environments. In these rich centers of exchange, new models emerge which embody a more awakened consciousness. Collaborative efforts among diverse perspectives and understandings give birth to new social forms and structures that serve the greater whole.

The Core Group Process™ is laying the foundation for a partnership model of empowered co-creative leadership. All individuals are seen as equal in the circle of life and valued for their unique contributions to society. Self-governance has replaced domination and control as individuals take responsibility for their choices and actions. The wisdom inherent in natural law creates the guiding principles for all nations. Leaders are coming together and accessing their collective wisdom as they make whole-systems decisions on behalf of all life for generations to come.

The power of prayer, clear intention, and group meditation is widely accepted and has been integrated into daily life in every sector of society. There is an experience of co-creation with all kingdoms of Earth, as ceremonies and rituals become integral to daily life.

The myth of scarcity has transformed into a recognition of, and appreciation for, life. New economic models that embody the values of caring, sharing, compassion, and recognition of unity have created a culture of contribution. Complementary currency, barter, local economies, multiple bottom lines, conscious consumption, and conscious investing have become the norm in our global culture.

Health and well-being are approached from a holistic perspective, as technological advances are interwoven with ancient tribal remedies to create a diversified inter-disciplinary approach to healing. The arts are flourishing, creating a global renaissance that cultivates a new narrative and propels humanity to the next stage in our evolutionary journey. Singing, dancing, and the performing arts are all expressions of celebration for the gift and the privilege of being alive! Media is transformed and is utilized consciously to inspire, uplift, educate, and inform.

It was with astonishment and delight during the era of the Great Turning that humanity experienced the emergence of a co-creative culture. It was as though there was an invisible root system quietly spreading throughout the land, activating a cellular knowing in social pioneers everywhere and weaving a beautiful tapestry of hope and possibility for all life on Earth.

Just as a butterfly delicately leaves behind its cocoon and soars into flight, the true co-creator—the new person—emerges as a fully conscious embodiment of Spirit's expression in matter, a perfect balance of the qualities of the divine feminine and the divine masculine. Humanity is opening its collective eyes and is being born anew.

SECTION 4

Staying Connected

Global Family

INSPIRE CO-CREATION

GLOBAL FAMILY, FOUNDED in 1986, is dedicated to supporting a shift in consciousness from separation and fear to unity, love, and co-creation. The mission of the organization is to empower and connect individuals and groups to actualize their purpose and co-create positive change in the world. Offering the Core Group Process™ is foundational to this mission.

By supporting the formation of Core Groups worldwide for three decades, Global Family has made the principles and practices of co-creation available to thousands of individuals and small teams in over 40 countries. This international network includes people everywhere who choose to experience themselves as members of one human family and to connect with others for the betterment of all.

A growing network of Ambassadors connects co-creators and supports local activities that honor diversity, foster unity, and allow individuals and teams to deepen in co-creative practices. The Global Family team at the United Nations collaborates with other non-governmental organizations to protect the rights of women, support sustainable development, eliminate poverty, and promote peace and social justice worldwide. (www.globalfamily.org)

Hummingbird Community

NESTLED IN THE Mora Valley at the feet of the Sangre de Cristo Mountains of northern New Mexico, resides a 486-acre ranch that is home to Hummingbird Community. Founded in 1996 by the co-authors of this *Handbook* and four other members of a Co-creative Core within Global Family, this spiritually-based eco-village is one of over 1000 intentional communities established in countries all over the world.

As social architects, community members are discovering and demonstrating a new way of living together. They aspire to align their values with their actions and support transformation in every sector of society. As emissaries of the new dream, they are creating an intergenerational sanctuary where every individual is honored as a divine being with unique gifts to share. Hummingbird members experience co-creation as the relational path to awakening. (www.hummingbirdcommunity.org)

Living Co-Creation

THE MISSION OF Living Co-Creation is to empower individuals and groups to express their full potential. In their work together, partners Carolyn and Sanford Anderson and Katharine and Makasha Roske share co-creative practices to foster personal awakening, enhance creativity, and fulfill a deep yearning for full Self-expression and the experience of true communion with others.

The innovative services offered include personal coaching and group consulting, experiential trainings and gatherings, and ceremonial services—all designed to equip change makers, social activists, entrepreneurs, and community builders to embody co-creative practices, discover and fulfill their unique callings, and contribute to birthing a caring, just society. (www.livingcocreation.com.)

Glossary

CO: Co in any word means "two things, one to the other joining" as in the words co-creation, community, collaboration, complimentary, cohesion, and cooperation.

CO-CREATION: going beyond cooperation and collaboration to consciously co-participate with the laws, patterns, or Impulse of Creation; conscious alignment with the Essence of others and with nature; Self aligning with Self, vertically and horizontally; a relational path to awakening.

CO-CREATIVE CORE GROUP: a group that comes together around a shared purpose that actualizes the gifts of all members and contributes to the betterment of society. Co-creative Core Groups usually evolve from Resonant Core Groups. (See below.)

CO-CREATIVE SELF: the Essential or Authentic Self expressing in the world.

CO-CREATOR: one who surrenders and aligns his or her will with the intention of creation, the designing intelligence, Spirit; one who joins with others in resonance to share his or her gifts to bring forth a new world based on unity and love; one who maintains attention on the consciousness force while engaged in action in the world.

CORE GROUP: an essential structure for personal and planetary transformation. A Core Group, or Evolutionary Circle, is a small number of people (typically 4 – 12) who are evolving personally and collectively and are contributing to the awakening of humanity and the betterment of society. (See the distinction between a Resonant Core Group and a Co-creative Core Group.)

ESSENTIAL SELF, AUTHENTIC SELF, THE BELOVED, THE SELF: The indwelling divine presence expressing as the individual; the infinite mind, Spirit, life, truth, and love which manifests in human form; the eternal aspect of humans.

EVOLUTIONARY CIRCLE: a small group who come together in resonance for the purpose of personal and planetary transformation; synonymous with Core Group.

HOLON: refers to something that is simultaneously a whole and a part. A human is a holon, as is an organization, a balanced team, or a community.

HOMO CO-CREATOR: the "new person" who is guided by soul essence, the desire to express unique creativity, and the vision of a world in which all people are free to give their best.

IMPULSE OF EVOLUTION: the creative force; divine intelligence; God; also referred to as the Impulse of Creation.

INNER COACH: the voice of the Essential Self; inner knowing or guidance; the internal guide in co-creating a new culture.

LOCAL SELF: the limited, self-conscious personality that may feel separate, alone, and in control; the ego operating in the world; also called the separate self.

MEME: an idea, belief or belief system, or pattern of behavior that spreads throughout a culture by repetition and replication in a manner analogous to the biological transmission of genes.

MORPHOGENETIC FIELD: a term used by biologist Rupert Sheldrake pointing to a new kind of information field where the collective memory or habits of past processes and structures reside and influence the present; the force behind the "hundredth monkey" phenomenon.

NOOSPHERE: a term coined by Teilhard de Chardin; the thinking layer of earth that surrounds the biosphere; the repository of all thoughts and emotions.

PRESENCE: awareness; consciousness; ground of being; the Essence of a human being.

QUANTUM THINK: a new system of thinking that brings together the basics of ancient wisdom and the brilliance of modern physics, allowing practitioners to live fully dimensionally, experience their wholeness, and harness the power of thought to co-create the reality they choose. For more, read *Do You Quantum Think?* by Dianne Collins.

RESONANCE: the invisible field of love in which co-creation occurs; resounding, echoing back and affirming the highest in one another; the frequency that aligns individuals heart to heart, calling forth the gifts and creativity of each person.

RESONANT OR RESONATING CORE GROUP: a group of individuals who align with the impulse of evolution and co-create an environment of accelerated growth; a sacred circle in which individuals experience unconditional love and connection with each other; a new social pattern in which individuals become one body with a collective sensitivity to the infinite mind and the will of the divine.

SPIRAL DYNAMICS: a developmental model of worldviews created by Don Beck and Christopher Cowan, building on the work of Dr. Clare W. Graves. This model refers to broad patterns of thinking as memes and provides a context for understanding co-creative practices.

SYNERGY: the interaction of two or more people that achieves an effect that is unpredictable and greater than what the sum of the individual actions can achieve; the effect that occurs when two or more are gathered in the name of truth.

WHOLE BEING: the full spectrum self: integration of the ego/personality and Authentic Self; the expression of our full potential at this time in humanity's evolution; the "new person."

To order additional copies of *The Co-Creator's Handbook 2.0*
go to www.globalfamily.org.

About the Authors

Carolyn P. Anderson

EDUCATOR, AUTHOR, SPEAKER, entrepreneur, and social pioneer, Carolyn is committed to the awakening of humanity to its full potential. Her passion is living and sharing the principles of co-creation and exploring the depths of embodied spirituality.

In her work with Global Family—as a co-founder and co-director since 1986—she has coordinated activities for numerous global events, assisted with the creation of social cooperation trainings, and facilitated a number of international conferences for adults and youth. (www.globalfamily.org)

During the Cold War, she brought groups of citizen diplomats to the former Soviet Union and Eastern Europe to create joint projects and be trained in co-creative practices. After the fall of communism, she initiated a "Feed a Family" program to provide meals for thousands of school children and pensioners in Moscow and St. Petersburg.

She has seeded hundreds of supportive Core Groups internationally to connect people at the heart and activate their creativity. In 1996 she co-founded Hummingbird Community in northern New Mexico as a "living laboratory for the evolution of consciousness and co-creation."

In addition to co-authoring *The Co-Creator's Handbook 2.0* with Katharine Roske, she has co-authored *Keeping the Promise, A Guide to Your Full Potential Self* with Rev. Jerry Farrell and is a contributing author to *The Change 4: Insights into Self Empowerment.* She co-created and edited the *52 Codes for Conscious Self Evolution* and the booklet *Birthing a Universal Humanity* with Barbara Marx Hubbard.

Carolyn is a partner in Living Co-Creation, a social entrepreneurial venture that offers training, coaching, and consulting in the practices of co-creation. She resides with her husband Sanford in the foothills of northern California. (www.livingcocreation.com.)

Katharine Roske

Social pioneer, educator, public speaker, ceremonialist and grandmother, Katharine is committed to the realization of a co-creative planetary culture that is a living embodiment of our spiritual essence. As a midwife for the new dream, Katharine has led her life on the evolutionary edge supporting transformation in many sectors of society. She is a founding partner and active steward of Hummingbird Community, a spiritually based eco-village committed to co-creative practices. (www. hummingbirdcommunity.org)

Katharine's professional career includes development and facilitation of programs focused on personal growth, co-creative community building, conscious evolution, empowered youth leadership, and women's spirituality. As a mother and grandmother of a large tribe, she is particularly passionate about supporting young leaders to express their life purpose.

She is a co-founder of the youth group, Earth Guardians (www.earthguardians.org), co-directed the Children's Torch of Hope Tour across America, co-founded a number of alternative schools, and has co-facilitated youth empowerment programs throughout the world. As an ordained minister she expresses her love for sacred ceremony by officiating at weddings, memorial services, birthing ways, land blessings, and seasonal celebrations. In 1999 she co-founded the Path of Ceremonial Arts for Women, a laboratory of the Divine Feminine.

Katharine is a partner in Living Co-Creation, a social entrepreneurial venture that offers training, coaching, and gatherings based on the principles and practices of co-creation. She resides with her husband, Makasha, at Hummingbird Community in northern New Mexico (www.livingcocreation.com).